Putting The Past Behind

Putting The Past Behind

Les Carter

Guideposts®

Carmel, New York 10512

Library of Congress Cataloging in Publication Data

Carter, Les.
    Putting the past behind / by Les Carter.
        p.   cm.
    ISBN 0-8024-6449-1
    1. Peace of mind—Religious aspects—Christianity. 2. Adjustment (Psychology)—Religious aspects—Christianity. I. Title.
    BV4908.5.C374   1989
    248.4—dc19   88-8037
                                                                        CIP

Printed in the United States of America

To my colleagues at the Minirth-Meier Clinic,
who have been a support and encouragement to me
for many years

Contents

Preface

It is often said, "What's done is done. You can't relive the past." That's true. No one can enter a time machine and rearrange prior events. But I am not sure this saying is entirely accurate. Though we cannot relive the past, we can take steps to overcome the pain our pasts bring into our present lives.

Virtually every working day I talk with hurting men and women who are living in the past. They are burdened with painful memories and hindered from knowing the joy and peace that is a by-product of faith in Christ. Instead they know fear, disillusionment, and insecurity. What is worse, some resist even the suggestion the past can be laid to rest. Using such excuses as "You don't know how bad it was," or "My habits are too entrenched to change now," they suffer misery every day.

God has given each person a memory — for a good reason. As the persons I counsel reflect on the experiences of the past, they learn from them in a way that positively impacts their lives in the present and in the future. Our memories were not given as a means of haunting us. God does not intend for us to hold onto past experiences in such a way that those memories create havoc in our lives. He is in the business of restoration and is only interested in helping His children grow away from the burdens brought on by sin. When the apostle Paul explained God's gift of salvation, he shared the wonderful news: "As Christ was raised from the dead through the glory of the Father, so we too might walk in newness of life" (Romans 6:4). By entering into a right relationship with God through Jesus Christ, we can rest in the hope of a new life. God allows us to remember painful experiences so that we can grow dependent on Him.

Yet many cry out, "I *have* accepted Christ as my Savior, but I still carry burdens from the past. Why doesn't my tension ease?" Usually the reason is that they have not fully understood that the difficulties they experienced in the past denied them basic God-given needs, a deprivation that in the years to follow resulted in various forms of tension coming into their lives. These persons are like the man who agreed to play a game of tennis before he knew the techniques and strategies of the game. He couldn't help having difficulty on the court. In a similar way, after conversion we each have much learning to do.

In counseling, I help individuals overcome burdensome tensions from the past by prompting them to gain an insight into the way their most basic needs were improperly addressed. Following that I describe the connection of unmet needs in the past to psychological tension in the present. I encourage the persons I counsel to absorb God's truth as it relates to unmet psychological needs: for every problem the world throws our way, God has a solution. Our task is to set our minds on the truth of His answers, then to make His answers so much a part of our thoughts that they supersede the painful memories of days gone by.

This book will unfold in a systematic way. First we will examine the five basic needs God has given each of us. This should prompt in you a sense of soul-searching as you seek to understand what your history gave you that was contrary to God's design. Then we will explore the ways unmet needs can produce the tensions of guilt, bitterness, and feelings of inferiority. Next we will look at God's response to our unmet needs. God is gracious: our every problem is met with a wonderful solution from heaven. Finally, we will explore how the manifestations of tension can be exchanged for contented living.

Though many feel defeated by struggles related to past difficulties, they need not despair. God has placed the Holy Spirit within each believer to lead him to the abundant life.

My prayer is that this book will find its way into precisely the right hands. My desire is that this book will help you find peace in God's love.

Many thanks are extended to Dede Johnston, who faithfully labored with me in the preparation of the manuscript. She has a gentle spirit and a willingness to serve and was a blessing to me during the time of writing.

Part One
Unmet Needs Produce Tension

ONE

OUR BASIC NEEDS

No adult can claim immunity from tensions in the past. A lifetime of exposure to the blemishes of sin ensures that. Some have suffered more than others, yet no one is completely exempt. On the dreadful day that the ways of sin were chosen over the ways of God, patterns of imperfection were begun and then passed along generational lines. To this day those patterns have not been eliminated. Anger consumed the firstborn son of earth's first family, and today the presence of undesirable emotions, poor communication, and bad behavior is evidence that sin's influence is still with us.

It may seem odd to begin a discourse on personal growth by declaring that each of us is doomed to struggle. Yet the acknowledgment of this truth is important because it forces us to appeal to God for the intervention we cannot manufacture within ourselves. Once when I talked with a woman about the certainty of personal suffering, she placed her hands over her ears and cried, "Don't tell me things like that. I can't bear to hear anything negative!" Sadly, this woman failed to understand that an admission of human frailties can be the beginning of growth. We should never be afraid to examine our weaknesses and vulnerabilities.

In spite of the certainty that we will each struggle, Christianity gives us hope in the message of salvation. Jesus said, "Come to Me, all who are weary and heavy-laden, and I will give you rest" (Matthew 11:28). Our God is merciful, and He does not desire that we carry burdensome tensions from the past.

Though sin brought us into defiance of God, causing us to experience painful consequences, God's mercy compels Him to pull us from the rubble of worldly stress. Our task is to discover how to allow Him to work in us.

Growth beyond past hurts is contingent upon our ability to identify the basic needs God created in us, to understand the way the world thwarts the fulfillment of those needs, and to see how our needs can be resolved through yieldedness to Christ. We must develop an understanding of human nature solid enough to ensure that as we work to change our behavioral and emotional patterns, we will be guided by a mind filled with God's truth. When we know His truth and commit ourselves to live in it, we become free from our painful pasts.

IDENTIFYING OUR BASIC NEEDS

The first step in overcoming problems from the past is to identify the key needs that are the most likely to lead to turmoil when they are not met. Certain needs are prominent in each person regardless of his national origin, religious persuasion, or the era in which he lives. By knowing those areas of greatest vulnerability, we can begin the process of knowing ourselves and of discovering how we can adjust to overcome our past.

THE NEED FOR LOVE

The most basic need of all is the need for love. In the first moments of life an infant cries out for someone to cradle him. We know that this craving for love is not learned or acquired because of the instinctive manner in which it is communicated. A child can detect when a parent has or has not properly responded to this need, and he can show by his reactions that he appreciates love once it is given.

This desire for love does not end when individuals mature into the later stages of life. Though each passing stage is distinguished by its own demands and tendencies, the need for love remains constant. It is this need that prompts teenagers to be particularly sensitive to the opinions of their peers.

It prompts young adults to desire a mate. It prompts parents to care about the activities of their children. It prompts us all to wince when we are rebuked or to smile when we are warmly embraced. Our need for love is evident in our sexual yearnings, in our wish to be affirmed, in our preference for pleasant conversation, and in our demand for respect. Not an hour can go by without each person's expressing in some reaction, thought, or emotion the desire to be loved.

When an individual consistently knows love, his behavior is likely to be responsible, his communication of himself to others appropriate, his emotions stable, and his capacity for spiritual insight heightened. When love is experienced, peace is found. That is why the primary thrust of Jesus' ministry was not the healing of the sick (though He healed many), or the teaching of doctrine (though He spoke as no other authority in history), but was instead the exhibiting of the love of God. All the aspects of His ministry that attracted attention were meant to illustrate His character as the One who came to address life's foremost need. He was aware that mankind's fall into sin created in each person a self-preoccupation that hindered the exchange of true love. Consequently, His entry into human history was intended to restore mankind to the love lost in the Garden of Eden.

It is no coincidence, then, that Scripture gives so much prominence to this need:

> Beloved, let us love one another, for love is from God. (1 John 4:7)

> This is My commandment, that you love one another, just as I have loved you. (John 15:12)

> If I have the gift of prophecy, and know all mysteries and all knowledge; and if I have all faith, so as to remove mountains, but do not have love, I am nothing. (1 Corinthians 13:2)

> Walk in love, just as Christ also loved you, and gave Himself up for us. (Ephesians 5:2)

Be devoted to one another in brotherly love; give preference to one another in honor. (Romans 12:10)

When love is not extended to a person, he feels that lack of love as rejection (fig. 1.1). The results can be devastating. I have counseled innumerable individuals who can refer to past experiences of rejection as the beginning of abnormal tension in their lives. Sometimes the rejection was subtle: an authority figure misunderstood them, they were made to feel that they had to perform if they were to be accepted, they were unfavorably compared to a sibling. But others recall more severe experiences of rejection. They were harshly criticized or verbally abused, they had relatives who loved alcohol more than family, they were the subject of sexual victimization and harassment, or they were entangled in bitter and unresolved disputes.

Figure 1.1

When individuals have an unsatisfied hunger for love, they become desperate for affirmation. Often they choose inappropriate means of finding that affirmation. Their social skills are blunted by underlying feelings of insecurity, and their defense mechanisms are too prominent. The inevitable result is even further deterioration in their primary relationships: possessiveness, insistence, inhibitions, anger, disillusionment, phoniness, shyness. Their emotional stability hangs by a thread, because their sense of contentment is too dependent upon the behavior of others.

THE NEED FOR FREEDOM

Suppose you stood on a street corner and asked one hundred people, "Do you believe freedom is superior to bondage?" You would find that the overwhelming majority affirmed the desirability of freedom, even scoffed at the notion of comparing the virtues of freedom to the defects of enslavement. Deep within the human spirit is a craving to be autonomous. Anything that threatens this autonomy people consider objectionable. All people—wherever they live, whatever their level of civilization—want to feel free.

Scripture introduces the concept of freedom in its description of the life of Adam and Eve in their garden home. God had told the couple that they could eat of any of the trees in the garden except for the Tree of the Knowledge of Good and Evil. That is to say, they were to let God be God and were to submit to His determination of ultimate right and wrong. Beyond that, they could live as they chose. God's desire for mankind to be free was so broad that He allowed Adam and Eve even the choice of whether or not to obey or disobey His commandment concerning the tree. But from the beginning, mankind was intended to have freedom balanced by faith in God. And even though our human parents made a great error in judgment, renouncing their faith in God, God continues to offer men freedom. Though His disciplinary love provides consequences for our choices, it does not negate the gift of liberty.

When freedom is present in relationships, acceptance of others is offered without preconditions. Demerit systems are not the rule of the day. Successful communication does not overemphasize regulatory lists of "musts," "shoulds," "can'ts," and "have tos." Responsibilities consistent with Scripture will be given prominence, yet they will be carried out by choice rather than by compulsion. In free relationships, individuals are allowed to feel what they choose to feel, think what they choose to think, and behave as they choose to behave. That is not to say that chaos or anarchy is condoned. Responsible freedom is balanced by consequences. It simply means that freedom in and of itself implies an absence of dictatorship and a presence of choices.

When individuals experience distress as the result of unpleasant events of the past, quite commonly they complain of a lack of true freedom, a lack of choice. This unmet need for choice leads to a feeling of confinement (fig. 1.2).

Figure 1.2

People who feel confined often recall past relationships that relied far too heavily on an authoritarian style of communication. Orders were frequently given, and options were rarely discussed. Correct performance was demanded, but little allowance was made for mistakes. Criticism was more common than mercy. The subjective side of life (emotions and unique perceptions, for example) was discouraged so strongly that repression occurred. Being right was more important than being loving. Fear, guilt, and hidden rebellion were thus encouraged.

THE NEED FOR INTERNAL CONTROLS

Freedom is a legitimate need we all have a right to have met, and satisfaction can result from a healthy dose of it. But in order to keep freedom from becoming chaos, we need inner controls. A well-conceived, Spirit-guided system of right and wrong is God's provision of checks and balances for the freedom He entrusts to us.

A lack of inner control is one consequence people experience as the result of difficulties they have had in days gone by. As adults they are faced with a myriad of decisions about emotions and relationships, but they find themselves floundering for direction. They don't know how to handle the complications of plans gone sour, and consequently they frequently experience frustration, worry, and guilt.

Interestingly enough, though, these people are likely to be the very ones who tell me that their past was full of instructions about what was right and wrong. If anything, they were overinstructed in these matters. They presumed that this overinstruction meant that they had no further need to contemplate a control system. But the weakness in such a past is that the controls taught were merely external. True discipline from within was not stimulated. One woman told me that she had always been taught to be kind and pleasant to people, yet she could not speak lovingly to her husband, especially when he made a mistake. We discovered that in her past she had regularly been told what to do but had never been given encouragement to consider for herself how she might best relate to others. Instead of being asked, "What are your ideas about communicating?" she was told, "Here's how I think you ought to handle this situation." Her system of controls was dictated by authority figures rather than being something she seriously thought about on her own. The result was a lack of discipline (fig. 1.3).

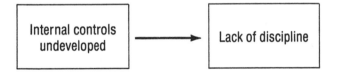

Figure 1.3

It is important that each of us be instructed in how to live, but it is even more important that we be taught how to *think*. The writer of Proverbs put it this way: "As he thinks within himself, so he is" (Proverbs 23:7). Our emotions, how we communicate ourselves to others, and our behavior are all stimulated by powerful guiding thoughts. If attention is not given to what those guiding thoughts will be, our lives will be guided by the impulses that naturally accompany indwelling sin. Although tense persons may be capable of intellectualizing about what they do or think, the root structure of their emotional system is not sufficient to provide the nutrition essential to bring forth good fruit. In many such persons this deficiency will exhibit itself in quicksilver moodiness. Others will resist structure and accountability. Still others, though less visibly hostile to controls, will have a passive resistance to what is right. They might know what God desires for their lives, but they will fail to exercise the discipline necessary to live that life.

THE NEED TO BE FAMILIAR WITH ONE'S EMOTIONS

From the earliest years of childhood throughout all adulthood we have emotions. Although some people express their emotions less openly than others, no one can claim exemption from the emotional aspect of life. God did not want us to be mechanical. He gave us an emotional nature that we might fully experience Him, each other, and His glorious creation. Galatians 5:22-23 explains that when His Holy Spirit indwells us, we have privileged access to His characteristics, many of which are emotional—love, joy, peace, patience, and gentleness. By creating us in His image and giving us emotions, God intended that through subjective experiences we might have depth and purpose in our lives.

Mankind was created in perfection, and thus we can assume that in the pre-sin days of Adam and Eve all emotions were pleasurable. Being perfect creatures in a perfect world, they had no impetus to experience troublesome feelings. But as soon as they succumbed to Satan's temptation to try to be as wise as God, they entered a dimension that included undesirable emotions. Immediately they became susceptible to fear, estrangement, guilt, and inadequacy. And because of this unsettled emotional atmosphere, the children of Adam and Eve developed anger so strong that one son murdered another. You and I might want to be free from the negative emotions Adam and Eve experienced, but we must acknowledge that as long as we are "in Adam" (1 Corinthians 15:22), we too will wrestle with those emotions.

In every generation from Adam to the present, most families have been ill at ease with negative emotions and have sought to cover them up by discouraging one another from expressing or exploring them. When someone in the family feels the emotions of fear or frustration, he is encouraged to stifle his feelings. He is not encouraged to explain why he feels the way he does or to find out what might have brought those feelings about. Consequently, it is all too common for individuals to stagger into adulthood with little or no experience in resolving their emotions.

What is equally distressing, many families feel insecure in expressing and exploring the *positive* emotions—love, tenderness, and contentment, for example. The result is that far too many adults do not have the emotional capacity for intimacy, even though they desire it. I have heard many discouraged adults express frustration that a parent or a spouse refused to share anything of a personal nature. These adults would agree that just as the repression of negative emotions has its ill effects, so too does the failure to exchange positive emotions. The release of laughter and excitement is as important to the fulfillment of needs as is the open exploration of discouragement, irritability, or anxiety. The net result of not becoming familiar with one's emotions is emotional incompetence (see fig. 1.4).

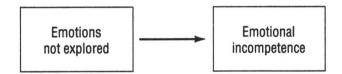

Figure 1.4

A person who has little experience in dealing with his emotions is likely to adopt a life-style that places too much stress on the objective aspects of life. Correct performance is so important to him that he accepts himself and others only conditionally. His spirituality leans toward legalism. He regards unique perceptions as invalid—conformity is what he demands. Gentleness and tenderness are awkward for him, and so he he finds it difficult to express love.

THE NEED TO CONTEMPLATE GOD

A truly successful life must be founded in a personal relationship with God through Jesus Christ. No matter how popular or how wealthy or how knowledgeable an individual may become, he is a wretched failure if he does not come to terms with the God of all creation. That is so because God did not create humanity only to turn His back on us in disinterest. He created us that we might have fellowship with Him. Though each of us lives in a body, we are spiritual beings first, created in His image. When our earthen vessels wither and die, our spiritual selves will still be left to reckon with God. Consequently, spiritual development is a need that must be fulfilled if someone is to be a growing person.

Beginning early in life and extending throughout adulthood, each individual needs to be stimulated to search for the truth that is of God. Everyone needs to contemplate the basic questions of life: Why did God create me? What does it mean to relate to Him? What is real success? What does it mean to be separated from God by sin? Why is there suffering? Not to meditate on such questions is to be vulnerable to expending energy on the self-serving aspects of life: performing strictly for personal gain, neurotically seeking human favor, focusing on temporal matters rather than on the eternal.

Invariably, individuals with troubled pasts will admit that they were not encouraged to contemplate God deeply. Often when I inquire about their knowledge of God, they reply that pertinent spiritual matters were either not discussed at all or were "pulled off the shelf" only when their parents gave them lectures about being good. The predictable result was that when they became adults they were frustrated by an inability to draw strength from the ultimate Source of power (fig. 1.5).

Figure 1.5

Because such persons have only a shallow knowledge of God, they hesitate to follow the biblical injunction to cast their cares on Him. He is not real enough in their minds. As a result, when human solutions are inadequate to resolve deep personal problems, they experience unwanted tension. Christians and churchgoers are not exempt from this problem, for in many cases the religious instruction they were given focused more exclusively on God's rules than on God Himself—their beliefs were *told to* them rather than being *developed in* them.

When God instituted the family, He specifically and deliberately gave parents the task of illustrating His character to their children. Likewise, He constructed the marital relationship to be an experiential picture of His love for us. Additionally, He created the offices of the church to be a reflection of His character to the world. In other words, because He loves us as His very own, God designed all the significant relationships in our lives to be mirror images of His compassion, thereby enabling us to know how to truly relate to Him. It is part of His perfect design. Yet the sin nature causes too many parents, spouses, and church leaders to abandon or to misunderstand their responsibilities in this area, leaving those in their care to find God as best as they can on their own. Consequently, when people who have never seen God's character illustrated in daily relationships most need God, they are likely to flounder in darkness. That is especially true of individuals who have been surrounded by insensitive people. Though they may have heard of concepts such as grace or forgiveness, because of the sour taste left in their mouths by the treatment they have received, they are unable to digest spiritual food.

THE CONSEQUENCES OF UNMET NEEDS

Each individual has basic God-given needs that must be met in order to nurture personal wholeness. If some or all of these needs are improperly addressed, the net result is tension (fig. 1.6).

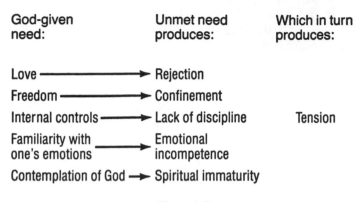

God-given need:	Unmet need produces:	Which in turn produces:
Love ⟶	Rejection	
Freedom ⟶	Confinement	
Internal controls ⟶	Lack of discipline	Tension
Familiarity with one's emotions ⟶	Emotional incompetence	
Contemplation of God ⟶	Spiritual immaturity	

Figure 1.6

Tension can be defined as mental and emotional duress that detracts from the contentment of God. This tension can be manifested in a variety of ways. In the first part of this book, we will examine five of the most common manifestations of the tension that results from a history of unmet needs: (1) a mind-set of distress, (2) a root of bitterness, (3) unresolved guilt, (4) dependence-independence imbalances, and (5) inferiority-superiority struggles.

When we familiarize ourselves with the manifestations of our tensions as they relate to our God-given needs, we will then be able to pursue solutions to those tensions. These solutions will be discussed in the second part of this book. They include: (1) developing the overcomer's mind-set, (2) yielding to God's sovereignty, (3) living in God's grace, (4) developing a life-style of balanced dependency, and (5) communicating coequality.

As we fortify ourselves with insights into the nature of our unmet needs and familiarize ourselves with principles of growth from God's Word, we will find assurance that it is possible to grow beyond many past tensions.

TWO

A MIND OF DISTRESS

Have you ever noticed how widely individuals can vary in their responses to a circumstance? Because each person begins with a different set of preconceptions, it is possible for two people to experience or observe the same event but formulate entirely different impressions of it.

As I ate a meal at our clinic's lunchroom recently, I was amused at the bantering that was taking place between two of our doctors. One of the doctors was in a playful, needling mood and was eager to share his glee with anyone nearby. Eyes alight, he was ready for feisty interplay. The doctor with him was more somber, and clearly he wanted to resist interaction. He was hesitant to speak and kept his eyes fixed into the distance. When he was forced to talk, his remarks were sarcastic and ever-so-brief. You see, their respective alma maters had played a football game the previous weekend—and you can guess why their moods were so different. The spry, happy-go-lucky doctor was on the winning team's side. To him, the game was a huge success. His bias for the winning team made him interpret the outcome in positive terms. The bias of his friend, however, led him to quite a different conclusion. To him, the game was a colossal failure. He saw nothing good in the event.

Although the outcome of a college football game can hardly be considered earth-shattering, the responses of the two men proves a point. Our emotional and behavioral responses to the events of life are dictated by the thoughts we allow to guide us. We are each the by-product of a unique mind-set. A mind-set can be defined as an intellectual filter system that guides a person's perception, understanding, and interpretation of life. Attitudes, prejudices, beliefs, emotions, and outlook are included in that mind-set. The mind-set we have dictates our response to the environment. A. W. Tozer captured this concept well: "The larger world cannot affect us directly; it must be mediated to us by our thoughts, and will be to us at last only what we allow it to be."[1]

Romans 8:6 summarizes how powerful the focus of the mind is: "For the mind set on the flesh is death, but the mind set on the Spirit is life and peace." Clearly, we would each prefer a mind of peace over death, but an individual whose needs were not met in the past may have developed a negatively skewed mind-set that makes it difficult for him to yield to the Holy Spirit.

Each working day in my counseling office I am aware of how important the mind-set of a person is. Some clients are open to insights and are eager to discover how they can make adjustments in negotiating personal struggles. The therapeutic interventions I attempt are more likely to be successful with these persons, for they are determined not to let the past bog them down. Other clients pose great difficulty. Their thinking is so pessimistic that they have convinced themselves that their problems are insoluble. They receive my therapeutic interventions halfheartedly, and they are unreceptive to insights that could change their lives. Their unmet needs have wielded too strong an influence in their thoughts and emotions.

When unmet needs gain a foothold in a person, the mind-set of that individual takes a decidedly negative turn. That is because our minds are designed to reflect the day-to-day encounters we have with those who are significant to us. If our experiences feed the mind messages that go counter to our God-given needs, our thinking patterns will show the ill-effects (fig. 2.1).

1. A. W. Tozer, *That Incredible Christian* (Camp Hill, Pa.: Christian Publications, 1964), p. 95.

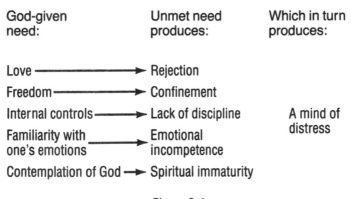

Figure 2.1

The first step in reversing the negative effect of unmet needs on the mind-set is to identify how unmet needs can shape the course of our thinking.

Rejection can cause a person to question self's capacities. When an individual is rejected often enough, he forms the impression that he is unworthy. Self-doubt becomes the norm. As he begins to assume that his opinions likely will be vetoed by more powerful others, he feels a sense of insecurity. Thoughts about his ineptness become dominant in his mind. His sense of isolation makes him feel different and even stupid. He assumes that there is no use trying to improve, for a lack of being loved has given him a "what's the use" mentality.

A woman who had never felt loved by her father and then was abandoned by her husband after sixteen years of marriage told me that she was sure her future would be miserable because she had no confidence in her relationships with men. The rejections she had experienced had caused her to assume a mind-set of defeat. She did not realize that she could think of herself as a competent person who happened to have been exposed to men who had problems in sharing God's love.

Confinement can cause a person to believe that he is unable to think through problems. By definition, confinement implies a loss of choices. Therefore, the individual repeatedly exposed to a restrictive environment is not practiced in sifting through the options available to him in emotional struggles. He is more likely to want easy solutions. When he is required to deliberate about sensitive issues, it is easy for him to say, "I can't." For example, an adult who was regularly denied the freedom to think about personal choices will quickly become pessimistic when he is faced with a particularly difficult circumstance.

Lack of discipline can produce mental laziness toward the struggles involved in personal growth. Since we each need training to develop internal controls, the person who lacks that training soon comes to believe that his life cannot come under his control. It is easy for him to become demoralized when the the environment forces him to work through his problems. Asking him to handle such a situation is like asking someone to run a marathon before he has had the chance to develop skill in long-distance running. An overwhelming mind-set of discomfort appears even before the effort is made.

Emotional incompetence causes an individual to feel threatened by the feelings that naturally accompany problems. When difficult emotions appear, he sees them as unmanageable. He has no well-conceived plan for dealing with anger, guilt, or fear, and therefore is likely to rationalize that he shouldn't have to be bothered by such feelings. In reality, his mind is accepting a posture of inability.

Spiritual immaturity inhibits the mind from developing a pattern of thinking that is founded on the Word of God. The need to contemplate God is so central to a mind of peace that to be denied this need guarantees a mind that is less than fully balanced. Even when spiritually immature individuals *do* seek God's ways, they tend to focus so heavily on God's *rules* that they do not draw sufficiently from God's *character.* Being grounded in external religion rather than internal spirituality, these people often conclude that God cannot be trusted to guide them.

Most persons who have developed distressed thinking patterns can identify one or more of these unmet needs at the base of their mind-sets. Knowing such information about their past is a vital first step for them in changing their lives.

Two Commom Mind-Sets of Distress

When individuals have a history of unmet needs, two patterns of thought frequently become prominent: the victim's mind-set and the defeatist's mind-set. Often there is overlap between the two thought patterns, for the mind-set of the victim easily leads into the mind-set of the defeatist. If a person is to grow beyond the thought pattern of either the victim or the defeatist, he will need to investigate both mind-sets more fully.

THE VICTIM'S MIND-SET

A victim can be defined as someone who has been unduly subjected to suffering, injury, or loss by another. Using this simple definition, we can surmise that virtually every person who experiences emotional turmoil is in some way a victim. After all, being the interdependent people that we are, we do not have emotional highs and lows in a vacuum. There is always a reason for stress, and it usually involves interplay with another.

On a broader basis, each person is a victim of sin's hold on the world. Before sin there was no stress, no disease, no natural disasters, no relational disputes. Life had nothing short of perfection to offer. Only after Adam's fateful decision to defy God did the earth come under a curse, and we each became vulnerable to painful relationships and personal insecurities. No one can escape the many after-effects of sin, no matter how innocent we may think we are. Inevitably, each person will suffer in some way at the hand of someone else.

Thus every person can in some way lay legitimate claim to the status of a victim. Some individuals, in fact, seem to defy the law of averages by an overexposure to unfair circumstances. But a distinctive psychological problem occurs when an individual so exaggerates his status as a victim that he feeds his mind with false beliefs about himself, the power of people in his life, and his ability to resolve his own struggles. Accepting a permanent label as The Victim, he negates the chance to grow in Christ beyond the troubles induced by an imperfect world. Individuals who take on the label of victim allow their identities to be dominated by the unfair treatment they have received. The result is that their minds are bogged down in prolonged ailing, depression, worry, and the like.

Interestingly, the apostle Paul, who surely had legitimate claim to the status of victim, refused to allow his mind to be tainted by such an attitude. Thus when he referred to the problems he had endured—tribulation, distress, persecution, famine, nakedness, peril, and the sword—he gladly proclaimed: "But in all these things we overwhelmingly conquer through Him who loved us" (Romans 8:37). He had concluded that though a person might indeed be a victim, he did not need to adopt the mind-set of The Victim, living in perpetual tension. In spite of ill treatment, we can become conquerors through Christ!

THE DEFEATIST'S MIND-SET

As a person begins to accept his status as victim, his mind further deteriorates into a defeatist mode. A defeatist is one who has succumbed to hopelessness, resulting in a feeling of personal ruin. The defeatist is characterized by chronic cynicism, bitterness, and disillusionment. The defeatist may have made many efforts to overcome problems from the past, only to fail because he presumes his circumstances are unique. He might be heard to say, "It's not as easy as you think."

At the heart of the defeatist mind-set is an ever-so-subtle form of grandiosity. This grandiosity is not so much of the bragging or conceited variety (although some defeatists are known to refer persistently to their problems as though they represented a badge of distinction). Instead it is born of the thought that no one else has ever been designated to suffer in quite the same miserable fashion. Armed with this mental focus, the defeatist can reject any helpful suggestions by claiming that his problems defy normal logic. The attitude is conveyed: "I know that other people have problems too, but no one can really understand what I've been through. I'm unique."

I know a man who experienced regular feelings of insecurity because of a history of being dominated by his father. His father regularly flew into hostile rages over the simplest matters. The son was subjected to instances of verbal abuse, and on a couple of occasions he was physically abused. As an adult, this man had difficulty relating to authority figures, particularly if those authority figures were ever impatient or opinionated. When the man's wife or friends suggested that he did not have to live in perpetual fear of being dominated, he would retort, "How can you possibly know how I should react? Have you ever been abused by *your* father?" Even when a friend intimated that he had been exposed to a similar background but had learned to thrive in spite of it, he shot back, "Well, you can't expect me to get over it like you did because at least you had good friends to turn to, and I didn't." It became clear that this man was determined to remain defeated by his past.

In a sense, there is a hidden "advantage" that compels the defeatist to hold onto such a mind-set in spite of the fact that he must also hold onto real pain. The defeatist mind-set excuses the individual from the vulnerability of examining personal issues. Driven by the feeling of insecurity, the defeatist prefers to avoid the risk involved in personal growth. He plays a subtle game of one-upmanship, in that he can claim a privileged status shared by no one else. He feels a hidden sense of superiority, which acts as a subconscious compensation for inferiority feelings brought on by past experiences.

PERPETUATING THE MIND-SET OF DISTRESS

Recognizing that unmet needs can prompt individuals to develop thought patterns of victimization and defeat, we should then seek to discover what individuals inadvertently do to perpetuate the mind-set of distress. Such a discovery could be instrumental in the individual's overcoming problems from the past since it would heighten his self-awareness. The following are four problems that keep a person mired in the victim's and the defeatist's mind-set.

AN UNWILLINGNESS TO ACCEPT TRUTH

As unpleasant as it is to admit, we must acknowledge that no one—no matter how good he is—is immune from unfair circumstances. Perhaps we could reconcile ourselves to the sad truth of suffering and pain if it befell only those evil souls who clearly deserve it. Coming to terms with problems is less easy, though, when it strikes an innocent person, particularly when that person happens to be *me*. Perpetually distressed persons tend to avoid accepting such truth, and in doing so they increase their agony.

The avoidance of truth is evident from the implied disbelief of the chronically distressed person. By clinging to past misfortunes he says, in effect, "I can't believe this happened! Surely this travesty was a mistake. I'm not supposed to be so exposed to such pain!" A mythical element is present in his thinking as he clings to a fantasy of unflawed living. Yet although such a fantasy creates temporary hope, ultimately it is destructive because it is based on a falsity. The person hopes to avoid the ugliness of suffering, but instead he is likely to be captured by diseased thinking.

More than 2,500 years ago, the prophet Jeremiah summed up human nature: "The heart is more deceitful than all else and is desperately sick; who can understand it?" (Jeremiah 17:9). The truth forces us to admit that man's sinfulness has set into motion a seemingly endless struggle with wickedness. (I say "seemingly" because we often lose sight of the truth that one day God will put wickedness to an end forever). Because the heart of man is desperately sick, we each are guaranteed interaction with people consumed by a propensity toward sin. And what is worse, we are each capable of creating problems for ourselves that may plague us for years. Sin is unattractive and cannot produce anything other than conflict.

Paradoxically, by admitting a vulnerability to sin's hold in our world, we take a major step toward escaping sin's power over us. Jesus Christ spoke to this point when He declared, "It is not those who are healthy who need a physician, but those who are sick. . . . I did not come to call the righteous, but sinners" (Matthew 9:12-13). If we lived in a spiritually and psychologically healthy world, Jesus Christ would not have come as the Deliverer of mankind. When people fail to face the reality of sin's infection, they cannot be soothed by the Great Physician.

THE DEMAND FOR REPAYMENT

Individuals hurting from past mistreatment understandably wish that old debts could be repaid. For example, a woman with an unsatisfactory history of daughter-father bonding will seek compensation through a loving husband. Or a man from a turbulent, angry background may place special emphasis on having serenity among his own children. Such a desire for compensation is not only normal, but it can be a healthy motivator to seek what is good.

Some individuals, however, perpetuate a mind-set of distress when they become excessively demanding regarding repayment of past wrongs. These people convince themselves that the past has denied their needs long enough; they have the right to preferential treatment. Brazenly accompanying such a person's sense of loss is a "chip on the shoulder." Even when others seem willing to be understanding and supportive, they maintain an edge of tension that creates adverse mannerisms.

Often individuals who live with the victim's and the defeatist's mind-set are not fully conscious of the excessiveness of their demands. That is, most do not plan at the beginning of each day to behave spitefully if their needs are unheeded. Yet there are common indicators of their subconscious motives: a hesitancy to draw close, a regular habit of criticism, stubborn resistance, uncooperative independence, quick skepticism, or one-upmanship games. Such tendencies reveal that they have chosen to live with a punitive attitude that "makes up" for old offenses.

One person who suffered in this manner was Helen. She was in her late thirties, and she might have been an attractive woman, but her face was set in a persistent scowl. From the moment she stepped into our clinic, she was rude to the secretary and abrupt with me. As I sought to ascertain her counseling goals, she pessimistically told me that she wanted to be rid of anger that had resided within her since childhood. But through her own admission she had never been able to make much progress because her snippy spirit made her an enigma to anyone who attempted to help her. I soon realized that her experiences of mistreatment in the past had caused her to become a demanding, aloof person who attempted to compensate for her unmet needs by relating to others in an overbearing fashion. Her negativism had become her way of staking claim to the right of "reimbursement" for a history of inferior treatment.

Although most people are not as blatant in their demand for repayment, anyone who has felt consistently mistreated is susceptible to this style of behavior. In a world that encourages competitive interplay, it is difficult to sidestep the temptation to exact some form of revenge.

ASSUMING AN ABSENCE OF CHOICES

When a person receives improper treatment, he characteristically feels controlled beyond his desire. In virtually any improper interaction, choices are withheld, and impositions are given. For example, a wife who has been subjected to a husband's insensitivity will recall feeling extra cautious about what she should say or do. Or a man who was teased as a child by his peers will remember feeling coerced into unpleasant compromises. An insecure woman with a history of family arguments will admit to moments when she felt incapable of doing the right things to soothe circumstances. When traumas are inflicted, many are so accustomed to feeling "put in their places" that they learn that they have no choices. Psychological paralysis results from damaged self-esteem.

In each life there are many things we cannot control. We cannot control what others do. We cannot fully control the presence of negative emotions in our personalities. We cannot control some of the random thoughts that torment us. But that does not mean we have no choices. We can control how we will respond to others' misdeeds. We can control how we will express our emotions. We can control the prominence given to individual thoughts. But the person caught in a distressed mind-set tends to focus primarily on what cannot be controlled rather than what can be controlled. This causes him to assume that one's ability to overcome is nonexistent.

As a teenager I often joked about my lack of mechanical aptitude. With a laugh and a lazy shrug I claimed that I could not be good at everything—and mechanics was one of the items on my "ineptness list." But in college and graduate school, I learned something amazing about myself. Being chronically short of money, I had to find ways to keep my car in running condition. By necessity I learned to do many mechanical chores I had once shunned: rotating tires, tuning the engine, cleaning the carburetor, changing the oil, installing brake linings. That forced me to conclude that my earlier claims of clumsiness were merely a cover for my lack of motivation to learn and to engage in a little hard work.

Similarly, when individuals claim that they have no options available to them in their circumstances, they are actually covering a lack of motivation for psychological and spiritual toil. Although these people are truly weary from the troubles heaped upon them, choices *are* available, though they may not necessarily be the preferred choices. The mind-set of victimization and defeat is only an excuse to keep the person from saying "I will," in place of the complaint "if only."

THE ABANDONMENT OF HOPE

Romans 15:4 tells us that the Scriptures were written that "we might have hope." Fully aware of our vulnerability to suffering, God has pursued us with the message of redemption from the strains our pasts have produced. But a person with a distressed mind has abandoned God's message of hope. Why is this so?

First, when we seek relief from the past, we often make the mistake of searching exclusively for external changes. For example, a disgruntled family member may confront relatives exclusively for the purpose of making them adjust their behavior. Or a spouse in a poor marriage may seek a divorce or begin an affair. It is true, of course, that external solutions are a necessary part of resolving hurts. But too often we so obsessively seek to resolve things in a way we can measure that we go overboard in our efforts. When we come to the end of the line, we either make poor external choices or we assume that hope is lost. Such an attitude discounts the fact that when external changes fail, internal solutions are still available. God has given each person a resource he can use when he is backed against the wall by earthly tensions: the guidance of the Holy Spirit. When we are guided by the Holy Spirit, we can choose to see beyond physical problems, grasping spiritual resolutions. Hope can thus be discovered through God's eternal perspective.

A second explanation for the abandonment of hope is our natural tendency toward pessimism. Because we are each sinners, we have inborn insecurities that cause us to expect the worst. Adam and Eve experienced this type of insecurity immediately when they fell into sin, and it impelled them to become afraid and hide. Deep within each personality is an awareness of human limitations. And when we attempt to resolve our needs by mere human means, we inevitably "hit the wall" of those limits. At this point many will concede defeat and conclude that life will never offer peace, thereby fueling a distressed mind-set within themselves. They do not nurture spiritual strength, thus leaving themselves bound to human limitations.

NEEDED: A MIND OF RESPONSIBILITY

When we experience problems from the past, we may for a time point with justification toward those who have provoked tension in us, reciting how our lives have been soured because of them. This reaction is not entirely incorrect, for our thought patterns are directly influenced by the unmet needs we have. But at some point—and the point varies among individuals and circumstances—the inflicted person becomes fully responsible to determine if the undesired event will or will not remain a controlling element in his mind.

During an exceptionally low point of his life, the noted Russian philosopher Alexander Solzhenitsyn was compelled to make a choice about the mental outlook he would follow.

He had been taken prisoner for disagreeing with the policies of the Soviet government, and he spent eight years in one holding cell after another, then an additional three years in internal exile. He was deprived of his most basic needs and was forced to endure a life-style not even befitting an animal. Yet near the end of his internment he wrote, "Live with a steady superiority over life—don't be afraid of misfortune, and do not yearn after happiness; it is after all, all the same: the bitter doesn't last forever, and the sweet never fills the cup to overflowing."[2]

Does this advice sound cynical? No, not really. Solzhenitsyn was merely trying to be a realist. Life's negatives are not permanent, so we need not allow our minds to be permanently ruined by them. Life's positives are pleasurable, but we cannot fix our hope solely in them, either. By living with a superiority over life, when we fix our minds on the things that are eternal we are capable of overcoming what is temporal. Colossians 3:2 echoes the thought: "Set your mind on the things above, not on the things that are on earth."

The implications of this belief are broad. Adult sons and daughters cannot repeatedly claim innocence for a mind-set of defeat or victimization just because their parents made mistakes in rearing them. At some point there must be a personal reckoning with God. Likewise, spouses who claim to be shackled with an insensitive mate cannot rightly sidestep the responsibility to love by stating that the partner will not properly reciprocate. Or a person seeking spiritual wholeness cannot excuse a mind-set of rebellion by explaining that he was treated poorly years ago by misguided church leaders. Eventually each person is responsible before God to choose whether his mind will be committed to God's guidance in moving beyond such problems.

2. Alexander Solzhenitsyn, *The Gulag Archepelago* (New York: Harper & Row, 1973), pp. 591-92.

THREE
THE ROOT OF BITTERNESS

When a person experiences tension from the past, the emotion standing above the rest is bitterness. When legitimate needs are lacking, disillusionment and dejection become strong, providing fertile soil for the seeds of bitterness. Left to grow unrestrained, this bitterness can turn any person into a pitiable wreck. Hebrews 12:15 instructs, "See to it that no one comes short of the grace of God; that no root of bitterness springing up causes trouble, and by it many be defiled." Admittedly, this instruction is not always easily implemented, but failure to weed out the root of bitterness ensures torment.

No one enters adulthood *planning* to feel bitter. As is the case with any emotion, it can creep uninvited into a life, spoiling one's intentions for upright living. When such an emotion appears in someone's personality, that can be interpreted as a signal that his basic needs have not been met. As we determine to respond to bitterness constructively, we can learn how to resolve our needs in order to conform to the will of God.

If we are to understand bitterness, it is helpful to examine the unmet needs at its origin.

Rejection creates in an individual the sense of feeling debased. And because each person has an innate self-preservation mechanism, that feeling of being debased makes a person want to stand up for his needs. If the perception of rejection is powerful enough, though, the individual feels that even these efforts at self-preservation are unheeded, and he begins to acquire a sour disposition. He develops resentment against the rejecting party, but because he "swallows" his feelings, he develops a growing sense of hostility.

Confinement causes an individual to feel throttled in personal expression. Like a pet who seeks to be released from its leash, the confined person has a profound craving to be set free. But when his efforts at becoming free are stifled, a bottled-up rage is born. He may make an effort to be compliant in what he does outwardly, but inwardly he feels defiance. The desire to rebel is strong, but the demand to conform squelches it. One man explained this sensation by saying, "I have lived my entire life feeling like I absolutely had to stay within proper guidelines. But in my thoughts I have been stepping over every single boundary." The emotion that expresses this feeling is bitterness.

The lack of internal controls leads to bitterness since the individual is uninitiated in the art of sorting out emotional options. Usually bitterness begins as a feeling of irritation that could be fairly readily resolved if it were examined immediately and thoroughly. But in most instances, when irritants arise, the person is not encouraged to think through his plans for resolving the problem, and so the irritant remains. As time passes, more irritants are experienced, and these are piled on top of earlier unresolved problems. Without a well-planned scheme for internally controlling each of these problems as they arise, the net result is a build-up of deep bitterness.

Emotional incompetence also causes a build-up of troublesome experiences. Each person is at some time going to experience fear, loneliness, guilt, and worry. But when one is not familiar with those feelings, they create in him an additional burden of frustration with himself and others. Just like the person who gets lost and then becomes frustrated when he negotiates the highways in a new city, the person who is inadequate in dealing with his emotions will sense an increasing anger. The longer this anger is unresolved, the more likely it will turn into bitterness.

Spiritual immaturity can cause a person to be so focused on the hopelessness of the human condition that he does not give proper attention to the hopefulness found in God's eternal plan. A lack of depth in the full knowledge and *experience* of God creates deep futility. This futility prompts cynical statements: "My suffering is more than I should bear. Maybe I can't really trust God." Or, what is worse, an individual may not even think anything at all about God and thus be engulfed with the things that are negative in human experience.

When our basic needs are unmet the result will be bitterness (fig. 3.1). Although it will do individuals no good to blame persons in the past for creating an environment conducive to bitterness, understanding the root of bitterness is part of the process of overcoming it.

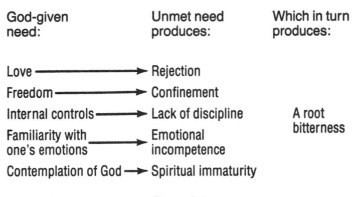

God-given need:	Unmet need produces:	Which in turn produces:
Love ⟶	Rejection	
Freedom ⟶	Confinement	
Internal controls ⟶	Lack of discipline	A root
Familiarity with one's emotions ⟶	Emotional incompetence	bitterness
Contemplation of God ⟶	Spiritual immaturity	

Figure 3.1

THE KEY ELEMENTS OF BITTERNESS

Bitterness is defined as profound grief accompanied by suppressed hostility toward seemingly unbearable circumstances. By including grief in this definition, the idea of loss and sadness is captured. And the recognition of hostility assumes pent-up feelings of anger.

To cope with bitterness, a vital first step is to distinguish its key elements. As an understanding of bitterness develops, plans can be successfully formulated to discharge it from one's emotional system.

UNRESOLVED ANGER

First and foremost, bitterness is a form of anger, the emotion of self-preservation that is instinctively aroused when one perceives he has been treated inconsiderately. Anger's basic function is to rally the individual to take a stand for his basic needs and innermost feelings of worth. Ephesians 4:26 instructs us to be angry without sin, meaning that we are to carefully consider ways to communicate our needs and convictions to those showing little respect for them. Then James 1:19 wisely cautions us to be "slow to anger," using restraint and discernment in the expression of our anger. Examples of constructive, biblical anger could include stating convictions in the midst of discord, saying no when necessary, requesting favors meant to meet legitimate needs, and confronting wrongs.

Unfortunately, many individuals are not well disciplined in anger. Too frequently they express anger through open aggression (shouting, criticism, griping) or passive aggression (silent treatment, laziness, sulking). They adopt these methods of expressing anger because they do not know the proper manner of expressing anger or because a constructive means of expressing anger seems unavailable to them. In either case, when anger is unresolved it takes root in the personality and gradually turns into the unsavory emotion of bitterness. Like a cancer it silently spreads throughout the personality, leading to emotional disease and spiritual damage.

The possibilities of anger turning into bitterness are plentiful:

• A child repeatedly receives condescending messages from an authority figure who does not allow the child to express dissenting thoughts or feelings. The child's anger is repressed and years later manifests itself through depression or rebellion.

- A wife feels persistently misunderstood by her husband. He makes no attempt to elicit, much less perceive, her unique point of view. She feels defeated, and feelings of disillusionment and despair fester within her.
- A worker encounters a work environment in which people are treated like objects. Unable to change jobs because of the economy, this person feels caged and becomes burned out.
- A man becomes weary of the moralizing he receives from family members. Distance grows in his relationships with them, and he takes on an "I don't care" attitude as he increases his level of alcohol consumption.
- A man has a knack for social skills and makes several efforts to befriend his neighbors. But when the neighbors feel no need to bring a new member into their clique, he feels hurt.
- A church member is dissatisfied with the direction the local church is taking in spiritual growth. He tries lovingly to share his concerns with the church leadership, but he is rebuffed and labeled a malcontent. He loses his desire to search out the Lord.

Because every person is a sinner and is not naturally predisposed to respond to conflict perfectly, and because people everywhere are prone to errant ways, the chances for debilitating anger are widespread. The longer we hold onto anger, the greater the possibility for bitterness.

At this point we should address the question, Is it wrong to feel angry? It all depends on sin's influence over the emotion. Originally mankind was not predisposed to anger. Before the Fall we had the capacity for anger, just as we had the capacity for sin. But we can confidently assume that before the Fall the only emotions experienced were positive. Anger is not mentioned in the Bible until Genesis 4:5, after the Fall. Therefore, because anger did not become part of our life-style until we became sinners, many conclude that anger is by definition a sinful emotion. But that assumption is only part of the picture. Although anger is not pleasurable, it can have constructive goals. In most cases, the bitter individual can recall a proper reason for feeling angry. That is, an improper circumstance produced the need for him to stand in defense of his God-given worth and needs. But because the heart of an individual is never totally pure, the positive reason for anger could be overshadowed as the person uses negative means to release it. When anger crosses the line into bitterness, it is helpful to seek a balanced perspective: Can the root of anger be properly addressed even as the individual remains committed to living within God's will?

SADNESS AND LONELINESS

Not only does bitterness contain elements of anger, but it also consists of sadness and loneliness. Bitterness is never experienced when understanding and camaraderie are high. Rather, it always has roots in moments of isolation and separation. Simply stated, no one experiences bitterness because of too much companionship and encouragement. The emotion is always undergirded by alienation.

Inevitably, bitter individuals can recall disillusioning isolation originating in relationships that did not live up to their expectations. Most commonly, the relationships producing the bitterness are the primary ones: parents, a spouse, children, close friendships, or work associates. Questions and disenchantment become prominent: "I thought we had a better friendship than this." "It just doesn't make sense that he would have treated me so poorly." "Why couldn't we sit down and work out our differences?" These thoughts easily grow into obsessions. Like a malfunctioning record player, the mind is stuck in one groove—it cannot move forward. The unexpectedly wide gap in relationships is perceived as a threat, and as the individual maintains an inability to move forward, his emotional disposition becomes worse and worse.

When lingering feelings of sadness and loneliness continue unabated, they indicate unsuccessful grieving—an inability to accommodate the reality of one's relational losses.

Although each of us would like to avoid losses in our primary relationships, the reality of sin dictates that failures will occur, sometimes with alarming harshness. Grief cannot be avoided. But bitter people have chosen to resist accepting this reality, and unwittingly their attitude causes their sad, lonely feelings to become more intense.

One man, for example, complained of bitter feelings toward his mother because she had adamantly refused to be sensitive to his needs. No amount of pleading would cause her to soften her manner of communicating herself to her son. For a lifetime, this son had felt deeply estranged from the one person he desperately wanted to love. But though his emotional turmoil originated from a primary relationship that offered loneliness, his bitterness was a result of his refusal to grieve successfully over the fact that their relationship would never be the way he had once hoped.

The distinction between successful and unsuccessful grieving hinges on accepting reality and trusting in God's willingness to carry one through disillusionments to a position of restoration. Although we may never embrace loneliness as a positive emotion, we can learn not to be threatened by it, thereby diminishing its power over us.

THE LACK OF CONTROL

Bitterness is also undergirded by the intense frustration of feeling undeservedly controlled. The bitter person frequently bemoans the fact that events have gone counter to his schemes, leaving his hands tied. Choices and options have been limited, with the consequence that the feeling of being dominated is omnipresent in the individual. Predictably, this person protests that he has been deprived of his God-given free will, but those protests are often met with resistance. The result is a feeling of futility.

To understand how the restriction of control can lead to bitterness, it is helpful to recognize that self-control can be either healthy or sinful. On one hand, self-control is listed in Galatians 5:23 as part of the fruit of the Holy Spirit's indwelling presence. Scripture repeatedly instructs us to yield our minds to God's will, acknowledging Him as the source of all that is good in us. When we do so, balance comes into our lives, and we are enabled to resist our sinful desires. The result is the type of control that brings order to a life once characterized by disarray and confusion.

But there is a desire for self-control that is sinful. Genesis 3:1-6 records the conversation between Satan and Eve in which he entices her to try to be like God. Satan's tactic was to encourage in Eve a self-preoccupation that would cause her to crave dominion over her own life. Eve succumbed to the temptation Satan placed before her. Shunning God's authority, she succumbed to a take-charge mentality God never intended for her. We are each Eve's children, and like her, we are tempted daily to yield to a craving for the type of self-control that is self-centered and rebellious toward God. The craving for control can thus be understood as a springboard toward a mind-set of self-centeredness. It is this type of desire for control that is an integral part of personal tension.

When the natural human need for the appropriate type of self-control is denied, a sinful desire for control takes over. An unloved son or daughter may fantasize about controlling the feared parent's behavior. A disillusioned employee may wish he had power over his boss' decisions. A rejected spouse preoccupies his mind with the changes he thinks his mate should make. These bitter people regularly repeat such phrases as, "I just wish . . ." or, "Why can't they. . ," or "If only they would . . ." Though these people may indeed rightfully claim that they have been unfairly controlled, paradoxically the more they crave control over those who wronged them, the more their emotions swing out of control.

DAMAGED SELF-ESTEEM

Every emotion, every behavior is a commentary on our inner feelings about ourselves. The bitter person's countenance indicates deep struggles in the area of self-esteem. The inborn gift of God's worth has been disregarded, and in its place has come much confusion over self's value.

Let us be careful to understand that self-esteem is a subject that must be treated carefully in the Christian community. We must avoid the humanistic notion that man is the ultimate creation and therefore deserves a type of love bordering on self-worship. Our persistent inclination toward sin proves that this approach is an egotistical falsity. Yet we must also avoid the opposite extreme of believing that individuals are worthless. God's pursuit of us shows that He believes we are valuable. A balanced view of self-esteem asserts that each individual deserves respect, not because of how well he performs, but because of the greatness of God's declarations.

When a person is filled with an emotion as powerful and negative as bitterness, it shows that he has poorly formed beliefs about himself. Either he feels so self-righteous that he cannot accept the notion that others do not adore him, or his thoughts about himself are so pitiful that he is overwhelmed by a sense of his worthlessness to others.

Invariably the bitter person remembers condescension from others that made him feel insecure and pessimistic. He might have experienced conditional acceptance or social alienation. Perhaps he was constantly bossed about, or others may have communicated a skepticism concerning his abilities. Because God's plan calls for self-esteem to be taught, as opposed to its being instinctively known, these experiences of condescension had the result of tainting the mental picture he had of himself.

What can give balance to such a person's self-esteem? The truth of the gospel. Jesus Christ, the perfectly righteous Man who paid the penalty for our sins, intervened before God on behalf of sinful mankind. He declared that any person who claimed Him as master would be reinstated to the position of respect that was lost when we became sinners. And because God so honors the pleas of His Son, He is pleased to grant them. When Jesus Christ thus presents us to God in His righteousness, God perceives us to be without blemish, just as Christ is without blemish. Isaiah triumphantly exclaimed, "I will rejoice greatly in the Lord, my soul will exult in my God; for He has clothed me with garments of salvation, He has wrapped me in a robe of righteousness" (Isaiah 61:10). When an individual reckons his personal value on the basis of Christ's righteousness, that becomes a springboard not for self-worship, but for God-worship.

Bitter persons need to make this beautiful truth an integral part of their thinking. In doing so they can have victory over an imbalance in thoughts of self that can only lead to emotional sourness.

NEEDED: A FORGIVING SPIRIT

Ephesians 4:31-32 emphasizes the necessity of resisting bitterness in favor of forgiveness: "Let all bitterness and wrath and anger and clamor and slander be put away from you, along with all malice. And be kind to one another, tender hearted, forgiving each other, just as God in Christ also has forgiven you." When most people read such words they think, *OK, that sounds like the right thing to do, but how can I possibly "put away" such a difficult emotion?*

It is not easy to put away bitterness because it is not natural for any of us—sinners that we are—to veto an emotion with our mental faculties. Yet that is exactly what Scripture prescribes. The ability to overcome bitterness in favor of a forgiving spirit will only happen as the mind is yielded to the Spirit's guidance. To accomplish that, I suggest a threefold process.

1. Acknowledge the futility of bitterness. I have never heard a person proclaim that his life has been enriched by the presence of bitterness. All persons agree that bitterness always detracts from successful living. Living with the root of bitterness is analogous to trying to row a boat with the anchor fully lowered. Little forward progress is made, and even then it comes only with tremendous strain.

God's instructions are always given with our best interests in mind. When He instructs us to set aside bitterness, we can believe that He does so because He knows that bitterness is emotional energy poorly spent. Though we may not be powerful enough to keep bitterness from appearing in our lives, God's admonition against bitterness clearly implies that we have the ability to sidestep it once we become aware of it. The willingness to agree with His assessment of bitterness makes us willing to seek His alternatives.

2. Be willing to act assertively when that is warranted. Once a person recognizes that bitterness is futile, he can attempt to address his personal needs accurately, so that he can confront the outward causes of his bitterness. He can accomplish this task through assertive communication. Assertiveness is the process of preserving self's worth, needs, and convictions in a constructive manner. It involves straightforwardness, yet not the type of straightforwardness that diminishes the possibility of God's love thriving in the encounter. It remains consistent with the scriptural concepts of "speaking the truth in love" and being "angry, . . .yet [without sinning]" (Ephesians 4:15, 26).

The individual can express assertiveness in a variety of ways, depending on personalities and circumstances at hand. He can express old hurts in a loving way with a family member, he share with his relatives how they can help to ease the pressure of his schedule. A person can elect to live in God's will in spite of others' refusal to do so. He can say no when it is necessary, can set personal boundaries and stick to them, and can share convictions when others are wrong. The intriguing thing about true assertiveness is that when it is exercised properly it does not have to be accompanied with a frown or a glare. It can be firmly communicated, yet with composure and respect.

There is one major catch that sometimes leads to less than satisfactory results when assertiveness is put into practice: not all individuals respond maturely when they are confronted with assertiveness, even when that assertiveness is exerted in the proper way. Instead of receiving the assertiveness open-mindedly, they react defensively. In such cases the assertive person must be careful to stay on track rather than getting bogged down in rebuttal or punishment. He must follow the course of wisdom and maintain his resolve to lay aside bitterness even when his assertiveness is unproductive. He can do that by exercising forgiveness.

3. *Allow forgiveness to become the desire of your heart.* It is no good to attempt forgiveness simply out of duty. I have known bitter people who have prolonged their misery by saying to themselves, *Well, I guess I have to forgive since the Bible says we are supposed to, but I surely don't want to.* When this thought is present, any effort to forgive is wasted.

Admittedly, forgiveness is not natural since it involves a humility foreign to sinful mankind. Human beings are competitive inherently and prefer to conquer their adversaries. Individuals who have been slighted are prone to focus their thoughts or feelings on ways of gaining dominance over those who have hurt them. Furthermore, American culture is built upon the concept of personal freedom balanced by judicial consequences. Our legal system recognizes—at least in theory —that when a wrong is committed a fair and proper consequence should follow. These ingrained ideas make it difficult for many of us to choose forgiveness over bitterness. It goes against our need for fair play. We want full payment for past wrongs, and we feel compromised if a "halfway" solution is suggested.

By definition, forgiveness assumes that there cannot be full compensation for a wrong, for mercy must be exercised if one's spirit is to be rid of foul emotions. Forgiveness presumes a willingness to look beyond our natural impulses and cultural philosophies. It focuses on the greater goal of imitating God. Setting his mind on things above (Colossians 3:2), the forgiving person acknowledges that life should not be controlled by circumstances in the earthly realm. Rather, he understands that we are spiritual beings first and should give priority to God's ways, even when those ways may require us to accept the presence of some loose ends in the resolution of our earthly affairs.

FOLLOWING THE ULTIMATE ROLE MODEL

The most unspeakable crime of man against man was the crucifixion of Jesus Christ. For some three years Jesus had built a tremendously popular following through His healing miracles, His abounding compassion for the lowly, His powerful teaching, and His ability to cleanse sinners of their shame. Though the masses were often confused regarding His mission and identity, they rightly speculated that He was the long-awaited Messiah. Wherever He went He drew a crowd. People loved Him, worshiped Him.

Our familiarity with the story of Jesus Christ reminds us that He was not without enemies. Because His popular message of redemptive grace threatened the legalism of the religious establishment, that establishment was relentless in seeking ways to discredit Him. Failing, they turned to the only other solution they could imagine—killing Him. After much maneuvering, they finally had an opportunity to act against Him, and they seized it. A mockery of a trial was held, and the religious leaders cajoled the Roman procurator, Pontius Pilate, into complying with their scheme.

Considering Christ to be demon possessed, the religious leaders treated Him contemptuously, spitting on Him and deriding Him. According to John 19:1, in the morning hours of the crucifixion day Christ was so severely flogged by His Roman guard, was so brutally beaten, that His physical features were not even recognizable. Isaiah 53:3 prophetically describes the coming Messiah as "one from whom men hide their face," a prophecy well fulfilled in Christ. His bloodstained body was so distorted by mistreatment that people were sickened when they gazed upon Him. Matthew 27:30-32 reports that Christ was beaten with reeds almost to the point of death. He was unable to carry His cross, and Simon the Cyrene had to be pressed into service on His behalf.

We can only imagine the pain endured by our Lord when the nails pierced His hands and His feet. Then He was subjected to still greater distress when the cross was hoisted into the air, His body torn by the jerky movement. Surely He must have been close to delirium. If anyone ever had a right to feel bitter, it was Jesus Christ at that very moment. There He was—the perfect Son of Almighty God, whose "crime" was to illustrate His Father's grace and mercy—yet he was being tortured and put to death by a haughty religious establishment and their band of thugs. The shame of such an act cannot be overstated.

What was Christ's response at that moment? Luke 23:34 reveals it. He said, "Father, forgive them; for they do not know what they are doing." Determined to set aside the temptation of bitterness, Jesus chose forgiveness. In doing so, He taught us how to handle our bitterness.

FOUR
UNRESOLVED GUILT

Although bitterness is a major emotional hurdle to clear in the effort to make peace with the past, guilt also figures strongly in troubled personalities. The impurities of living engender in humans the desire to be cleansed before God and man. This effort to right wrongs is certainly appropriate, for refusal to do so would constitute the condoning of sin. However, because many are confused about how to accomplish cleansing, their efforts to resolve guilt are often incomplete, leaving them with an improper devaluation of self.

God wants us to accept His offer to remove our guilt because He wants us to appreciate fully His loving character. The first step in living without debilitating guilt from the past is to become aware of the ways guilt can gain a foothold in our personalities. We can bring about that awareness by learning the way our unmet needs create in us a tendency toward feeling the emotion of guilt.

Rejection deprives individuals of the feeling of value that is vital to inner stability. When we are rejected, it is difficult for us to find the contentment prescribed in Scripture for those who are in Christ. Instead, we often feel useless and worthless. That can lead us to accept too much blameworthiness when an error occurs or a relationship fails. We think, *Since others don't think well of me, maybe I really am a bad person.*

Confinement is another element that causes a person to have a poor evaluation of himself. When an individual is forced to live in a restrictive environment, he commonly perceives himself as incapable and untrustworthy. Also, since a confining atmosphere tends to be characterized by a heavy emphasis on duty and obligation, the confined individual is commonly dominated by the emotion of fear, which in turn causes chronic self-doubt. Persons living in an atmosphere of confinement are likely to become preoccupied with the requirement of living within prescribed limits, thereby heightening their feelings of failure when mistakes occur.

Lack of discipline becomes an underlying contributor to guilt when an individual has not developed a plan for handling the complexities of living. When difficulties occur he wallows in feelings of ineptness. A man once told me how he had struggled with shyness. Because he had not developed communication skills, he blamed himself when conflict or awkwardness occurred. We all know that a measure of internal control is necessary for responsible living. When this need is unmet we feel shame because of our inability to alleviate or overcome problems.

Emotional incompetence in an individual will lead him to the emotion of self-blameworthiness when he fails to negotiate emotions successfully. Most people know that worry or anger or impatience can and should be handled maturely. When an individual lets these emotions go out of bounds, he is likely to experience excessive shame in the aftermath. He may thrash himself with self-talk: *You're going to have to get a better handle on yourself! I don't know why you can't control your feelings any better than this.*

Spiritual immaturity is probably the greatest contributor to unnecessary guilt, because the person who is not accustomed to drawing strength from God is going to find it difficult to accept the concept of forgiveness. Since God is the ultimate arbiter of right and wrong, a failure to be familiar with His grace and sovereignty displays itself in insecurity.

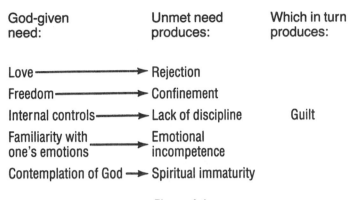

God-given need:	Unmet need produces:	Which in turn produces:
Love ⟶	Rejection	
Freedom ⟶	Confinement	
Internal controls ⟶	Lack of discipline	Guilt
Familiarity with one's emotions ⟶	Emotional incompetence	
Contemplation of God ⟶	Spiritual immaturity	

Figure 4.1

IS GUILT GOOD OR BAD?

In the past few decades, there has been a great movement toward guilt-free living. Though people are as prone to guilt now as they ever have been—as witnessed by the continuing reality of unmet needs—our "enlightened" modern thinkers actually encourage us to disregard guilt. Tired of ethics they think of as stodgy and too pristine, humanistic activists have succeeded in convincing the general public that sin is acceptable. Disdainfully rejecting Judeo-Christian principles of decency, they have argued that people should behave however they wish and should feel free to adjust their thoughts and emotions to suit their whims. Morality, they reason, is relative to individual preferences.

To illustrate how far our culture has moved in this regard, consider the changes that have occurred in television in the past thirty years. Three decades ago a wide array of family programs featured themes suitable for young children to enjoy with their parents with no fear of embarrassment or violation of human decency. But within the time span of one generation, the air waves have become flooded with prime-time programs that feature sex without benefit of marriage, provocative clothing, drug addiction, homosexuality, free use of foul language, live-in relationships, teenage suicide, seductive music videos, and a general disregard for authority.

What has happened? In the name of reality and openness (which are actually lies and lewdness), today's humanists have convinced the public that guilt and moral accountability are outdated. Self-indulgence is now the norm. Secular humanists argue that when we feel shame or blameworthiness, that does not mean that our behavior is wrong, but rather means that our attitudes are old fashioned. So instead of being encouraged to respond constructively to guilt, we are given permission to change the rules. In the book *Whatever Became of Sin?*, Karl Menninger observes that

> in all of the laments and reproaches made by our seers and prophets, one misses any mention of "sin," a word which used to be a veritable watchword of prophets. It was a word once in everyone's mind, but now rarely if ever heard. Does that mean that sin no longer is involved in all our troubles—sin with an "I" in the middle? Is no one any longer guilty of anything?[1]

Quite accurately, Dr. Menninger argues that a life that ignores the correcting influence of guilt is a life destined for misery.

Indeed, guilt is a necessary emotion and has a useful function. Sinners that we are, we need an internal alarm system to warn us of the corruption that accompanies indwelling sin. Properly experienced, guilt is a feeling of blameworthiness that prompts an individual toward constructive adjustment. It calls him to a healthy self-scrutiny consistent with Psalm 26:2: "Examine me, O Lord, and try me; test my mind and my heart." If we do not allow the Lord to examine us in this way, we become prisoners of Satan's schemes and philosophies.

When we examine sins from the past, a healthy sense of guilt encourages in us prayers of repentance and reliance upon the mercies of God. Yet, as with so many other helpful

1. Karl Menninger, *Whatever Became of Sin?* (New York: Hawthorne Books, 1973), p. 13.

traits, guilt can become so exaggerated that it is more of a hindrance than a help. When past problems are too prominent in a person's present life-style, he can be drained of joy and effectiveness for God. When that occurs, false guilt has probably gained a foothold. Therefore, it is helpful to learn to avoid the extreme of false guilt while at the same time maintaining the healthy use of true guilt.

KEY ELEMENTS OF FALSE GUILT

As I mentioned, when one or more of our five basic needs is unmet, the true guilt of reconciliation is likely to be overshadowed by the false guilt of self-degradation. In order to right things, it is helpful to know what indicates that an imbalance in guilt has taken place. Once a person knows the symptoms and their immediate cause, it is possible for him to move toward freedom from this form of tension. The following are some manifestations of a personality shackled by excessive guilt.

A LEGALISTIC MIND

Foremost among the causes of false guilt is a legalistic mind-set. Legalism is the strict, literal adherence to the law, and it produces a burdensome sense of obligation in the legalistic individual. The legalist is so concerned with external performances that the internal motivations he has for what he does are poorly developed. When a legalistic individual is pressed to explain why he does what he does, he may be capable of reciting philosophic ideologies, but in truth he performs because of a sense of duty. For him, fear is a more powerful motivator than true belief. He is a slave to rules and regulations.

It is easy to see how individuals can adhere to legalistic living. Most of us can remember the messages we received in childhood regarding obligations. At home, at school, and in church we were regularly told what performances were required. We learned early in life that if we were going to thrive, we had to obey the rules. Now it *is* necessary to teach children rules—but it is also necessary to teach children to understand for themselves the reasoning behind the rules. That is where legalism falls short. Fearing failure and desiring approval, we as children learned to perform our way into good standing. And when we made errors or felt undesirable emotions, we learned to cover up. The letters a college student writes to his parents are more likely to emphasize the things he has done that are right than they are to emphasize the things he has done that are wrong.

Because of the sin nature, every person experiments with the "other side" of life. Some people are more blatant in their rebellion than others, but everyone can recall when he or she tested the limits. Most people at some point in their lives question their parents' ways, question the value of religion, and see authority figures as a nuisance. But when guilt begins playing its role of encouraging repentance, many individuals return to the childhood habit of doing what the authorities say is correct out of a sense of obligation. Although these people might once again be able to recite the rationale for moralistic living, in truth the corrective measures they adopt are more of a performance designed to "prove" their adequacy than they are activity motivated by deeply contemplated desires.

The most obvious representatives of legalism are the New Testament Pharisees. Once when they argued with Jesus about His theology, Jesus replied, "Everyone who commits sin is the slave of sin. . . . If therefore the Son shall make you free, you shall be free indeed" (John 8:34, 36). Jesus' good news was that we no longer have to be burdened by the yoke of performing correctly to find peace with God and with ourselves. His shed blood on our behalf made us free to focus on the fuller life motivated by our love for God. His rules of right and wrong remain, but legalism can be set aside in favor of an internal rather than an external motivation to live correctly.

THE REPAYMENT MENTALITY

One of my earliest memories is of an incident that occurred when I was about five years old. I was playing outdoors when I saw an older boy, probably ten years old, shatter the neighbor's garage window with a rock. Spotting me in the distance, he threw his head back and laughed heartily, then ran away. I thought, *Hey, he sure looks happy. I think I'll have some fun just like he did!* So I gathered as many rocks as I could and went to the neighbor's garage—which was separate from his house—and at close range proceeded to break the rest of the windows. Not satisfied by merely putting a hole in each pane, I threw rocks until every bit of glass was knocked loose from the frames.

Pleased with my effort, I went home and, being totally naive, immediately told my parents of the fun I had had. "You did *what?*" they screamed. I was amazed at their reaction. The older boy I had seen seemed to enjoy his rock-throwing activities. I was ordered to walk with my dad to the neighbor's house to explain what had happened. The neighbor was gracious as he listened to my story and seemed cooperative when my dad explained that he would assume full responsibility for the damages. When we returned home I was spanked, given a lecture, and told that I would have to work to pay for the repairs my behavior had made necessary. It was then that I learned that when sin is committed, a price has to be paid.

Virtually every adult can recall some similar episode from the past that taught him the lesson of retribution for wrongs. Consequently, all of us hold to the philosophy of keeping the slate clean and not being morally indebted to others. It is this philosophy that is behind the efforts spouses make to bend over backwards to show repentance after a great crisis. Similarly, it causes friends to return favors after they have received special acts of kindness. And it can prompt Christians who want to prove their loyalty to God to become heavily involved in religious programs. When the practice of keeping a clean slate has the motive of true love, the philosophy is good, and it is consistent with Romans 15:2: "Let each of us please his neighbor for his good, to his edification."

But though a legitimate need exists to keep a clean record of service to others and to God, a problem evolves when we do not keep the practice in perspective. It is possible to assume that we *must* perform endless good deeds for God in order for Him to erase our demerits. This erroneous thinking is the consequence of imagining that humans are capable of appeasing God. When we adhere to such a philosophy we become easy targets for false guilt, for it will only be a matter of time before our performances prove to be less than adequate. The inevitable result will be insecurity in our relationship with God and the collapse of effort to perform good deeds.

If we were capable of appeasing God through payment, Jesus Christ would not have needed to die sacrificially on our behalf. The law would never have been superseded by faith. Grace and mercy would be mute traits in God's character. The fact that Jesus did die for us, fulfilling the law, and that grace and mercy are poured out from heaven proves that our Creator recognized the need to institute a system of reconciliation to Him that was not contingent upon our feeble good deeds. Although our love for God should always prompt a desire to correct wrongs, we can set aside the propensity for false guilt by recognizing that those performances can never come close to earning eternal favor with God.

COMPARATIVE THINKING

One night I was awakened by a phone call from a frantic mother who told me that her twenty-one-year-old daughter, a client of mine, had been taken to the emergency room after an apparent suicide attempt. The next morning I visited the daughter in her hospital room. Candidly she told me how she had argued the day before with her parents about her failure to find work in a career-oriented company. She had stormed out of the house angrily, protesting that her parents had never accepted her and shouting her determination never to see them again. Just a few hours later she took an overdose of prescription medicines. Though the damage to her physically was minimal, clearly her depression was quite real. After talking with her about the incident and lending her some much-needed support, I asked her to see me in my office after she was released from the hospital.

Several days later we sifted through the factors that led her to feel so desperate that she wanted to die. Interestingly, Barbara referred to herself repeatedly as a failure, though it was clear over the years that in the eyes of many she was highly successful. Beginning in her grade school years she had consistently been selected as the most popular and most beautiful girl in her class. She had won many talent contests and had been selected head cheerleader. She had been elected an officer of her class. Throughout her teen years she had more dating opportunities than she knew what to do with. After graduation she had gone to college and had continued in the same vein of popularity and achievement. A superficial glance at her life's story might cause one to conclude that because she had always compared quite favorably with her peers, she certainly should have no problems with depression and despair.

But closer examination revealed that these favorable comparisons led to Barbara's fall. Through the years she had received so much pressure from parents, teachers, and peers to be the best, that she felt terribly guilty if she let anyone down. If chinks appeared in her armor, she concluded that she should live in shame. Her suicide attempt was her cry of protest against comparative pressures.

We can trace this tendency to try to be better than others to mankind's fall into sin. When Satan enticed Eve and Adam to be like God (Genesis 3:5), he fed them a lie: "Although you may not yet be elevated like God, if you apply yourself you can become at least His equal!" He knew that Adam and Eve's pride could be pricked in a way that would cause a competitive spirit to burn within them. And even though they quickly learned how dreadfully wrong Satan had been, Adam and Eve were not willing to let go fully of the lie. When God confronted them they immediately began playing a game of one-upmanship with each other in the attempt to shift blame. Furthermore, we read in Genesis 4 that their sons continued the game. When the oldest felt that he did not compare favorably to his brother, he killed him. The need to come out on top can be that powerful.

Being "in Adam," each of us has succumbed to the same temptation to be graded above others. That is illustrated by our willingness to second-guess God and by our pleasure in gaining special status over our peers. Then, just as Adam and Eve passed this mentality to their sons, we too pass it to successive generations. Our children are taught early in life to think in comparative terms and to find ways to stand out above the crowd. This explains our neurotic attention to physical appearance, good grades, being the winner, and living strictly according to the rules. Fully immersed into the comparative mind-set, we waste emotional energy that could be applied toward loving, godly pursuits. The net result is susceptibility to false guilt.

HUMANIZING GOD

About ten years ago I taught a Sunday school class of fifth grade boys. Over several successive Sundays I taught a series of lessons on heaven and the second coming. Because their young minds had not yet developed the capacity for abstract thought, their conceptions of life after death were quite interesting. To them, heaven consisted of baseball games in which they were able to hit a home run each batting turn. They assumed that in heaven they could order a Big Mac any time they pleased without having to pay for it. Summer vacations would last all year long. And best of all, there would be no kid sisters because the girls would live in the girls' section! When I asked how they pictured God, they shared images of a white bearded man in a bathrobe who had a couple of angels following Him around in case He needed someone to run an errand. He would be nice to them, they said, but you'd have to make sure you were good so that you wouldn't upset Him.

I chuckle to myself as I remember the way my class described God and heaven. Such innocence can be both humorous and refreshing. But sadly, I am reminded that many adults are not much more advanced than those fifth graders in their conception of God. Many children, teenagers, and young adults have had such inadequate instruction regarding the character of God that their images of Him are based mostly on images they have of earthly authorities such as parents, pastors, and Sunday school teachers.

Quite commonly, adults misconstrue God as the unseen Authority Figure in the sky who is more powerful than any other authority, but who has just as many quirks and idiosyncrasies as any human. God is pictured as a master statistician who keeps records of every good or bad deed committed. Then —depending on the final scores—He rewards the doers of good deeds by giving them a new luxury car to drive in heaven for eternity and punishes the doers of bad deeds by throwing lightening bolts at them. People ascribe human traits to God that portray Him as someone who plays favorites, holds silly grudges, and requires bribes before He will extend forgiveness.

Especially prone to such misconceptions are individuals who were exposed in the past to harsh parents or to harsh religious figures. Having learned how difficult it is to please humans, they generalize by assuming that God must be the same, and in so doing they humanize God. Although they are right to recognize that God has assigned parents and church leaders to represent His nature, they wrongly ascribe to God the failings of these people. They overlook the fact that just as a senator might misrepresent his constituency, so the human agents of God might misrepresent God.

Humanization of God fuels the possibility of false guilt, for a humanized God would be prone to the same peevish judgments as humans. Security would thus be undermined, for if God cannot be trusted, no sense of absolutes exists that might provide a foundation for true security. Uncertainties would flourish regarding the possibility of ever being forgiven of wrongs. Ultimately, a sense of defeat would prevail, for such a God would have to be humored and pampered to keep him from turning against someone if by chance that person provoked him.

Persons with erroneous thoughts about God need to restructure their ideas about Him, for spiritual thoughts do influence emotional reactions. Only as our thoughts of God conform to Scripture can efforts to balance guilt succeed.

NEEDED: BALANCED SELF-EVALUATIONS

We have recognized how unmet needs create undue struggles with guilt, and we have examined how guilt is often manifested. Armed with such awareness, we can rightly conclude that if we are to experience guilt in the proper way we need to adopt a balanced view of self based on the unwavering truths of Scripture. We need to integrate two major ideas into our thinking patterns.

The first is that *repentance is a vital part of emotional healthiness.* Second Corinthians 7:10 says, "The sorrow that is according to the will of God produces a repentance without regret." Since sin is ugly and is a part of our lives, we would be in error if we never lamented its consequences. God wants each individual to assume full responsibility for the wrongs we have committed and to apologize for them. As we do so, we are drawn closer to Him, for our repentance causes us to yearn after His character. Interestingly, though, He wants us to repent "without regret." That is, He wants us to learn from our mistakes but not at the expense of all self-esteem.

The second is that *judgmental thinking can be replaced by descriptive thinking.* People overwhelmed by false guilt have become too preoccupied by grades. Once they have made an error, they worry about the degradation forthcoming from humans. In doing so, they are inconsistent with biblical teachings that tell us to focus on God's opinions over man's. Second Corinthians 10:12 states that people who are consumed with concern regarding human comparisons are "without understanding." Romans 2:29 describes the true servant of the Lord as one whose "praise is not from men, but from God."

The thrust of Jesus Christ's ministry was to communicate the idea that in spite of what we do or how negative a grade our critics give us, God desires to draw us into His love. John 3:17 eloquently states, "For God did not send the Son into the world to judge the world, but that the world should be saved through Him." The only one fit to judge is God Almighty, and even though one day He will require of us a final day of reckoning, He prefers not to pass condemning judgment on us. This means that while human feedback and exhortation are productive, human judgments have no place in the mind and emotions of those who belong to Him. Judgment belongs to God and God alone.

Therefore, rather than being consumed with concern about grades, it is better to let our self-evaluations be descriptive ones. Rather than accepting human declarations of excellence or lowliness, we should learn to think through what is right and wrong, make emotional and behavioral adjustments, and then let God be the judge. After all, His opinion is the only one that counts.

FIVE

DEPENDENCE-INDEPENDENCE IMBALANCES

I often hear people explain how emotionally independent they are even when I can see much evidence in their lives to the contrary. Most individuals assume that if they are capable of being decisive or if they tend to keep their emotions private, they have no problems with dependency. But such assumptions merely indicate a limited understanding of this characteristic. Emotional dependency is defined as the tendency to allow moods and reactions to be controlled by external matters. A truly emotionally independent person, therefore, is one who is consistently stable in spite of his surroundings. Even if a person is independent in many tasks, dependency problems are indicated if undesirable emotions are too easily aroused by his environment. Independence of behavior is not always a reflection of independence in emotions.

Dependency is highly susceptible to being out of balance when the five basic needs are not sufficiently met. Either the individual becomes a "clinging vine" who must have approval, or he develops an unhealthy detachment from and disregard of others. To bring balance, it is important to understand how unfulfilled needs influence dependency.

Rejection leaves individuals with insecurities not easily conquered. Because the need for love is so elementary to our ability to relate satisfactorily to one another, when love is communicated conditionally or does not seem to be offered at all, we are likely to become preoccupied with the opinions of others. Some individuals attempt to resolve such insecurities by "bending over backwards" to please in hopes of getting pats on the back. Others are wary of their ability to sway opinions, so they remain aloof, not allowing themselves to run the risk of vulnerability. In either case these individuals are reactors who spend too much energy adjusting their behavior to the ways of others.

Confining experiences deprive individuals of the freedom to explore for themselves who they will be. Since confinement is evidenced by a heavy emphasis on duties and obligations, individuals who have been under this burden tend to be more concerned about the criticisms they might receive than they are in developing authenticity. These people are very sensitive to the standards of authority figures, and their stability is undermined if someone rebukes them for being out of bounds. They are likely to react to their situation by becoming either extremely sensitive or defensively aloof.

Lack of discipline created by a lack of internal controls also causes an individual to become a reactor rather than an initiator. Because emotional independence requires well-conceived ideas about handling problems and stress, when this inner guidance system is not present, the individual is susceptible to allowing circumstances dictate the course of his life. When internal controls are weak, persons will be controlled by externals.

Emotional incompetence leaves a person vulnerable to dependency imbalances, for his inability to negotiate feelings leaves him groping in sensitive moments. The individual who does not know what to do with his emotions will either instinctively look for someone to create emotional stability for him, or he will try to avoid the emotions altogether through some form of withdrawal. That is analogous to the practice a schoolboy might adopt if he were unfamiliar with his math homework. Either he will beg for someone to bail him out of the assignment, or he will quit altogether and declare the work nonsense.

Spiritual immaturity has much to do with dependency issues, for our beliefs about God are vital to our ability to control our moods. When we are spirituality mature, we depend on God for inner strength and do not allow circumstances to dictate our inner being. But when our knowledge of God is weak, or when it is more "book knowledge" than experiential knowledge, our inner moods are swayed by worldly strains (fig. 5.1).

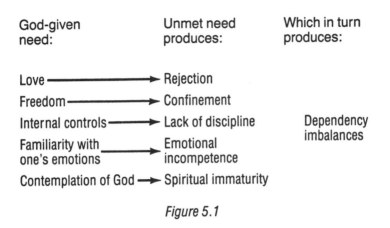

God-given need:	Unmet need produces:	Which in turn produces:
Love ⟶	Rejection	
Freedom ⟶	Confinement	
Internal controls ⟶	Lack of discipline	Dependency imbalances
Familiarity with one's emotions ⟶	Emotional incompetence	
Contemplation of God ⟶	Spiritual immaturity	

Figure 5.1

Because our temperaments and backgrounds vary, not all of us will manifest this imbalance in the same way. Yet this tension is always manifested by moods that are either too easily contingent on immediate circumstances or that are too detached or aloof from one's surroundings.

DEPENDENCE AND INDEPENDENCE SHOULD COEXIST

Dependency is by no means an abnormal personality trait. In His infinite wisdom God gave each of us this trait as a sort of glue to hold relationships together. No one can claim total independence, because inside each of us is a need to relate to others and to share love. God wants us to be drawn toward one another and toward Him in love, and dependency is the mechanism that causes us to do so. Our objective is not to eliminate dependency but to keep it in balance.

Likewise, independence is a normal personality trait. Because God wants to relate to each person as an individual, He has given each of us a craving to be separate from the crowd. By developing a sense of separateness, we establish uniqueness in our relationship to Him as well as to others. To underscore the healthy aspect of independence, God made sure that no two humans look, sound, or think exactly alike. (As a twin I can really appreciate that.) God wants each of us to have a distinct character, marked by distinct thoughts and life-styles. But as is the case with dependency, He wants this independence to be kept in balanced perspective. It is to be coexistent with healthy dependence.

Given the fact that dependence and independence are both healthy traits when they are experienced in balanced proportions, we can assume that deliberate effort should be made to develop these two qualities during an individual's formative years. But it is here that many people find impurities of development, leaving them vulnerable to responding to their basic needs with tension.

Developmental psychologists identify two necessary ingredients for balanced growth in dependence and independence: children need satisfactory love relationships that give them consistent and reliable messages of security, and they need to be specifically trained to handle struggles on their own so that personal competence can be instilled in them before they reach adulthood.

Childhood can be divided into three general stages, each stage having a distinct function in creating dependence-independence balance. Because of mankind's collective sinfulness, no one will develop perfectly through these stages. You do not need to be alarmed if your past did not unfold as it should have—God will still provide ways to find balance. Yet it is helpful to be aware of the ideal development sequences, for such knowledge can give insight into the ways your basic needs may have been unmet, culminating in adult tension.

In the first stage of life—the preschool years of infancy to six—dependency is at its peak. The majority of the child's needs revolve around the desire to be loved and affirmed. The child depends on his parents for food, shelter, and clothing, but even in meeting those needs, the parents' primary task is to make the child feel wanted. The child should be stimulated by frequent touching, holding, eye contact, and one-on-one play time with each parent. Studies have shown that infants and toddlers who do not receive sufficient stimulation can eventually exhibit learning deficiencies, social withdrawal, and extreme insecurity. Therefore, the importance of consistent nurturing during this time period cannot be overstated. As language development begins and motor skills become more refined, the child will become less inclined to cling to his parents for long periods of time. He is ready then to learn how to do simple tasks or to learn basic ideas. Nonetheless, the need for persistent affirmation remains dominant.

The second general stage takes place during the elementary school years—from about the child's seventh through twelfth birthdays. During these years the child enters a period of transition. He is still dependent upon his parents for security, and his thinking is concrete. Direct parental guidance in issues of right and wrong are still necessary. But during those years it is healthy for the child to venture into social activities, forming fairly strong attachments with individuals outside the home. The child's parents have the responsibility to continue offering affirmation, but they gain the additional challenge of teaching the child to see himself as a separate and distinct individual who has the capacity to make choices that will lift him above stress-producing circumstances. For example, when a nine-year-old boy complains about his whining sister, he needs the affirmative understanding of his parents, but he also needs encouragement to think through ways he might handle his frustration so that it does not get out of hand. In receiving such a message from his parents, his dependency needs will be satisfied at the same time the idea is being instilled in him that he needs to begin thinking independently about his habits of life, thus developing a proficiency of his own.

During the third general stage of life—the teenage years and the onset of abstract thinking—a major need of the child is to learn to contemplate who he is, what he believes, and how his guiding thoughts can help him resolve interpersonal and intrapersonal conflicts. Although he still needs support and affirmation, the child must also be encouraged toward greater independence by learning to conceptualize about his relationship to God and the implication of that relationship in regard to personal security. Parents need to work with their child to help him define his own sustaining philosophy of life, which will include developing strategies for negotiating emotions and relationships. The parents and child need to discuss how to communicate oneself to others, how to define love, and how to respond to temptation. When this kind of communication takes place consistently, by the time the child enters the adult years he will have developed personal stability, for he will have been given love and affirmation consistently, and he will have been able to develop personal competence. Dependency will still be a part of the individual —evidenced by a continuing desire for affirmation—but it can be balanced by an independent inner strength.

The problem experienced by most people is that their childhood did not unfold so neatly. Most adults experiencing emotional tensions can recall times when affirmation was not offered in sufficient amounts—either they were given too little affirmation or they were smothered by affirmation. And almost invariably people have received little encouragement to think about philosophies of relating to others or about methods of developing personal composure. Consequently, many have entered adulthood with an imbalance in their dependence-independence habits, causing them to be either too clinging or too detached.

EVIDENCE OF DEPENDENCE-INDEPENDENCE IMBALANCES

Flaws in our upbringing can create tension that takes the form of our being too dependent or too independent. Part of relieving this tension is to identify ways this imbalance can be manifested.

UNPREDICTABLE EMOTIONAL RESPONSES

As a college sophomore I was required to conduct simple experiments with laboratory rats to gain firsthand knowledge of learning patterns. Although at the time I thought my efforts had absolutely no applicability to my professional goals, I have since learned otherwise. In one experiment I trained a rat to press a lever in order to receive a drop of saccharin. I discovered that if I reinforced this behavior after each successful effort, the rat soon became content and directed his attention elsewhere. But when I required the rat to push the lever at least twenty-five times before I offered him a reward, he became far more anxious. He began to realize that he could no longer accurately predict when the reinforcement would occur, though it would surely occur sometime. With intermittent reinforcement he was reduced to a mind-set of uncertainty, and his emotional state was thereby more easily swayed by my whims.

In the same way, when our basic needs are sufficiently met we become capable of handling stresses in rational ways. But when we have learned to feel uncertain about what to do with what the world offers, we maintain a higher edge of tension and become more frantic in our responses to the environment. An individual who has been left to guess how he will handle the dilemmas created by unmet needs is most likely to develop an insecurity that is evident in the wide-ranging emotional struggles he endures. One day he is calm and collected; the next day he might be edgy and irritable; and the day after that he might be easily discouraged or depressed. Because of needs that were not fulfilled, his moods are too easily controlled by externals.

AN ANSWER-SEEKING MIND-SET

When we have not been fully satisfied in the meeting of our basic needs, we enact a type of searching for answers. Because we do not have a full measure of inner stability, we yearn for someone who will relieve us of our worries. In part, this tendency can be normal and healthy. But when it is carried to extremes, such searching creates more problems than it alleviates. Many persons are so accustomed to looking outwardly for direction that they barely develop an inner guidance.

The debilitating aspect of this habit was clearly illustrated for me by Myra, a woman in her early fifties who was still struggling to be freed from the effects of growing up in the home of a mother who was a chronic worrier and complainer. Throughout her adult years Myra had learned to keep peace by acquiescing to the decisions of others, just as she had done as a girl with her mother. Myra sought counseling because she knew she could not feel stable as long as she allowed others to decide how her life would unfold. Yet in spite of her resolve, whenever I asked her to think about the adjustments she would like to make in her life, she displayed a dependency imbalance. Instinctively she threw the question back to me: "What do *you* think would be best?" I knew that if I answered it would only perpetuate the problem, so we resolved together that we would not fall into such a trap. I encouraged Myra to act on her own ideas rather than chronically soliciting my advice.

When individuals seek the opinions of others too frequently, that indicates the presence of feelings of inadequacy. The solicitor is subtly communicating, "I'm not confident in my ability to resolve dilemmas. You'd better bail me out." They assume that they do not have personal proficiency or true trustworthiness. The result usually is that they experience such persistent struggles with frustration, fear, and anxiety that they can never be certain that their own notions are truly in their best interest.

BECOMING DISTANT

God has given each person a tendency toward human interaction. By temperament, some persons are more sociable than others, yet no one can claim that he began life with no inclination for personal interaction.

Sometimes when a person's basic needs are not satisfactorily met, he responds by becoming too distant. Perhaps he will even declare himself to be unconcerned about the opinions and feelings of others. In many cases such a person rationalizes that this mode of living is as normal as any other, thereby "excusing" himself from personal attachments. But just as the tendency to be too tied to others is inappropriate, so too is the extreme of withdrawing from relationships.

The tendency to be distant is often exhibited through rebellion, anger, or cynicism, and it often results in loneliness and depression. Many times people who are overly distant have self-destructive patterns of behavior, including alcohol and drug abuse, social isolation, or workaholism. Lacking the background that would have fully trained them in the qualities necessary for balanced relationships, they opt for more impersonal ways of living that will not require the effort to become personally vulnerable.

The distant person's problem is not easily resolved. On one hand, the history of minimal deep personal interaction has caused his desire for some form of affirmation to grow. But on the other hand, lack of success in relationships has produced in him a pessimism that causes him to think, *Why should I attempt to get close to people? It could fail.* In order to bring balance to their lives, these individuals need to make persistent efforts to become involved in others' lives. They need to recognize that when they make an effort to initiate relations, awkwardness may indeed be present, but that does not mean that they should retreat into old patterns of withdrawal and inhibition. They can choose to persist in seeking out close relationships, secure in the knowledge that God desires us to relate to each other in His love.

DESIRING INDULGENT TREATMENT

I don't know many people who will claim that they never want to be treated in a special way. We each have times when we prefer to be pampered. Only the most hardened persons will assert that they never want the red carpet treatment. Such a preference, when kept in proper perspective, can be quite normal.

Some individuals' need for indulgence, though, is so consistent that it clearly marks an imbalance in the dependence-independence trait. They desire nothing but ideal circumstances in which few if any real stresses are present. They not only dislike having to struggle with the routine problems of normal living, but they demand that they not be required to stoop to the level of work that their circumstances bring. When such a mind-set is present, it is obvious that the individual has not enjoyed the benefit of having his five basic psychological needs fulfilled. His craving for privileged treatment is a cry of personal weakness.

It might be tempting to assume that the persons most likely to suffer from this tendency are the wealthy. We could cite Matthew 19:24, in which Jesus states that it is more difficult for a rich man to enter heaven than for a camel to go through the eye of a needle. Jesus knew that spiritual growth requires the willingness to let go of earthly dependencies in favor of a humble life founded in faith in God. But to suggest that the wealthy are the only ones who have a desire for indulgent treatment is to hold too narrow an understanding of the trait.

Regardless of socioeconomic status, many individuals have not learned to develop inner strength and security. They feel the need for others to prop them up. For example, a husband who never talked with his parents about personal issues may demand that his wife keep personal problems to herself and treat him like the king of the castle. Or a woman who has a longstanding habit of allowing her emotions to rule may hold her family responsible for maintaining her fragile sense of composure. Or an adult whose family members were extremely attentive may expect others to treat him in the same way.

The weakness of such a tendency reveals itself when these individuals show themselves to be ill-equipped to handle the struggles that come into their lives. They exhibit anxiety, depression, and anger because they assume that they should be immune from common problems. They are convinced that others are responsible for the woes they experience, and they believe that the blame for their stress lies at the feet of those who refuse to be as perfect as they should be. The dangers of such a trait are twofold: it places others in the impossible position of having to fulfill a godlike role of caretaker, and it precludes the possibility of the individual's developing true depth of character, since he views struggle only in negative terms.

A WEAK GOD IMAGE

Ultimately, if a person is to find balance in the area of dependence-independence, he needs to develop a strong image of God. When an individual has a powerful knowledge of and reliance on God, he will have a strong desire to remain attached to people, because his goal will be to become a servant as Christ was. Yet he will be detached from others in that their opinions are not all-important to him; he will see acceptance from others as secondary to God's love. In contrast, when a person has an imbalance in his dependency needs, he shows that he has a weak image of God. When God created Adam and Eve, He intended that they depend solely on Him for psychological and spiritual wholeness. His perfect plan has always been that we be completely immersed in His character, satisfied in knowing that He is the complete source of stability. But when Adam and Eve fell into sin, their spiritual focus was taken away from God and placed onto the world. Likewise, if people today are not specifically trained to know God and His ways, their minds will fix on unnatural sources of wholeness.

Konrad Lorenz was an animal researcher famous for studies of imprinting. A number of years ago he observed that newborn ducklings immediately identified with and followed the first living creature they saw, which was usually the mother duck. For experimentation purposes Lorenz decided to remove the mother duck and hatch his own brood of ducklings, thus allowing the ducklings to identify him as their mother. Sure enough, when the newborn ducklings hatched, they willingly followed him wherever he led them, completely relying on him to show them what to eat and where to go.

People who have not had their God-given needs met in their early years are like the ducklings who imprinted on the wrong object. Since each of the five basic needs is designed to draw a person closer to God's character, the lack of fulfillment these people experience results in a weak understanding of God and His ways, leaving them vulnerable to the influences of worldly ways.

NEEDED: ATTACHMENT-DETACHMENT BALANCE

Keep in mind that dependency is not entirely wrong. Our moods and reactions will always be swayed to some degree by external matters. For example, when I am with friends who demonstrably love me, my mood lifts, but when I am amidst unfriendly critics I become guarded. It is normal to be influenced by circumstances. But my dependency would be out of balance if I insisted that people absolutely and always love me and never criticize me. At that point my inner composure would be too closely linked to environmental factors.

At the same time, we must bear in mind that independence is a good quality, though too much of it can be unhealthy. That is, we can so determine to rise above circumstances that we refuse to become involved in the everyday pressure of relating to others. Galatians 6:2 tells us to "bear one another's burdens, and thus fulfill the law of Christ." A refusal to become involved in others' lives is sin.

Balance comes about when we allow for both attachment and detachment in our relationships. Although on the surface this principle may seem to be contradictory, it is not intended to be. We can accomplish balance in our relationships by willfully becoming involved in others' lives while simultaneously determining that no human be given the power that should be God's to control our feelings of fulfillment. Although our lives will still be affected by interaction with others, we can determine not to be so dominated by another that the environment ultimately dictates the way our lives are shaped.

Without question, the greatest example of a person who lived with this balance was Jesus Christ. Scripture repeatedly depicts Him as One who became emotionally attached to those around Him. His healings were highlighted by a tremendous compassion. He was known to weep with friends who were bereaved. He was moved by the innocence of children. He shared in the happiness of wedding ceremonies.

Even His moments of anger showed that His mood was affected by the insensitivity he saw in man's disregard for his fellow man.

But there were also times when Jesus drew himself back, both physically and emotionally. At times He removed Himself from His disciples. At other times He and His disciples withdrew from crowds. When the crowd's expectations of Him became too intense, He refused to go out in public. And at His mock trial when He was spitefully treated, He remained mentally separated from the harassment of his captors, though He was physically present. As the picture of perfect balance, He knew that if He was to accomplish the mission given to Him by the Father, He could not allow His mood to be swayed by the circumstances about Him. Our goal is to imitate His exemplary life.

SIX

INFERIORITY-SUPERIORITY STRUGGLES

Every human begins life with a propensity toward experiencing struggles with a sense of inferiority. Being born into sin, we each live with the uneasy feeling (both conscious and subconscious) that we cannot maintain God's standard of perfection. Romans 1:18-20 indicates that each person is given an inner revelation of God's ways, which is to say that each of us is prompted in his conscience to know the essentials of what we should be, and that each of us is "under conviction" regarding our comparative status to God. We can understand how this works by observing young children, who instinctively know when they have done something wrong. They turn their faces in shame when a parent attempts to talk with them about misbehavior. They become quiet and withdrawn when they do not want a misdeed to be uncovered. Before they break a rule, they glance to see if an authority figure will spot them. These common, simple actions tell us that the children already are responding to an instinctive knowledge of God's ways, and that they are aware of their tendency to fall short.

A major task in personal development is to learn how to respond adequately to God's standard of right and wrong, and to know how to handle the inevitable emotion of inferiority when we do not meet His standards adequately. Specifically, each person needs to learn that although he is indeed inferior to God's perfect criterion, he does not need to be burdened with the false notion that one human being can be proved to be either inferior or superior to another. Although each individual is in desperate need of a Savior, no individual should compare himself to others in order to determine his own relative value.

When the five basic psychological needs are not adequately met, however, a balanced perspective is missing, and feelings of inferiority abound.

Rejection creates a feeling of insecurity, and repeated rejection can cause a complex to develop. The need for love is crucial to a person's sense of well being, and when love is communicated conditionally or does not seem to be offered at all, the individual naturally doubts his standing compared to others. He already possesses some feeling of insecurity by virtue of his sinful state, and rejection reinforces the idea that his value is limited. What is worse, when self-doubt grows through such experiences, he may become oversensitive to any hint of disfavor from others, resulting in his developing a fearful and defensive nature.

Confinement can add to the problem of inferiority by causing a person to feel that his efforts to develop personal competence are being squelched. When individuals feel compelled to conform to a rigid agenda of rules and regulations, they become so programmed to worry about errors that they experience a heightened feeling of inadequacy when they miss the mark. Also, when people observe others who are permitted to live more freely, they develop a persistent tendency to compare themselves unfavorably.

Lack of discipline feeds the problem of inferiority since the individual with undeveloped inner controls is naturally prone to errors in judgment. In each life, circumstances are bound to occur that require well-conceived ideas. But when ideas and philosophies are poorly formulated in one's mind, an inability to cope with life adequately will surface, followed by frustrated feelings of personal despair. Persons whose need for discipline was not met often complain of feeling awkward in the face of trials. When trials come they flounder with uncomfortable emotions, or they go out of their way to avoid struggles.

Emotional incompetence is at the heart of inferiority feelings because emotions cannot be avoided. When an individual is ill at ease in responding to another's emotions, or when he is required to sift through his own emotions and cannot do so adequately, he feels inept. Quite commonly people with this difficulty will not admit openly that they have feelings of inferiority because their emotional incompetence causes them to refrain from discussing such struggles. Nonetheless, their insecurity is demonstrated by the inadequate way they respond to personal matters.

Spiritual immaturity encourages inferiority, for the only sure way to be lifted from struggles with inferiority is to find acceptance from God. When individuals are hindered from the habit of truly comprehending how salvation reinstates people to a position of esteem, the messages of Scripture do not seem real enough. They have not internalized concepts of God's empowerment and guidance to the point that they are bolstered from the onslaughts of the world. Consequently, the spiritually immature person feels that he must rely on his own efforts to prove his adequacy, but he finds this that method of obtaining a sense of adequacy is frustrating because of the ever-present influence of his own sin nature (fig. 6.1).

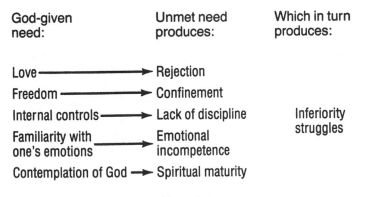

Figure 6.1

Knowing how easily struggles with inferiority can be aroused will prompt us to learn more about the problem so that we can grow beyond it.

Is It Ever Right to Feel Inferior?

Two extreme schools of thought exist regarding feelings about self. The self-effacing school suggests that it is wrong for an individual to think well of himself. Generally founded in legalistic religious beliefs, this tendency asserts that any form of self-love is sinful pride. And since "pride goes before destruction" (Proverbs 16:18), the people who hold this position assume that a valuation of self will lead to grave consequences. They see a feeling of lowliness as a refutation of pride. But though there is some legitimacy to this concept, problems can erupt when individuals adhere so strictly to the notion of lowliness that they have little or no base of security on which to build.

The more liberal extreme is represented by the humanistic school. Persons holding this viewpoint assert that man is the crown of creation and should therefore never be encouraged to accept low feelings about self. They describe self in the most glowing terms and believe the mind should be trained in predominantly positive self-talk. They shun any notion of human devaluation and encourage people to view their sinfulness as a frustrated reaction to a lack of valuation from others. But there are problems with this point of view, also, for the mind-set of an individual can be so puffed up that he feels no need to seek out God's empowerment.

The only reliable source of arbitration between two such differing philosophies is the Scripture. In the Bible we find two seemingly conflicting trains of thought coexisting with each other. On one hand, the abject lowliness of humanity is clearly taught, indicating that indeed we have reason to feel inferior. It is undeniable that no human being can claim moral superiority, because all persons have a natural proclivity to sin. Isaiah 64:6 speaks the unflattering message: "For all of us have become like one who is unclean, and all our righteous deeds are like a filthy garment." Even when we attempt to live correctly, our efforts are so short of God's high standards that we cannot possibly claim true superiority. Therefore, we would be remiss if we did not admit our lowly status.

On the other hand, Psalm 8:5 describes man as crowned "with glory and majesty." Being created in the image of God, our personalities are indelibly imprinted with a part of His character. We have been graciously gifted with the capacity to share love and to be conformed to His will. And although this glory and majesty is not made fully manifest until we become yielded to the Holy Spirit's empowerment, it is an integral part of what we are. Therefore, a type of self-love can be quite appropriate.

When we combine these two diverse teachings from Scripture, we find perspective regarding the inferiority struggle. It *is* proper and healthy for us to regard self as lowly and humble at the same time we rejoice in the truth that God has honored us with His glory in spite of our inadequacies. Such a beautiful truth keeps us from succumbing to a weary feeling of self-debasement, but also keeps us from claiming a sense of moral superiority. Though we are inferior to God's perfect design, we are not inferior to other humans, for God regards us equally. Acts 10:34 underscores this point declaring that God is not one to show partiality.

When persons have lived in an environment that has not met the five basic needs, this balanced conclusion is likely to be missing. Commonly individuals coming from such a background will lean toward one end of the spectrum or the other. Therefore, if we are to come to terms with the teaching of Scripture on this subject, we need to identify the ways we might exhibit an imbalance in our thinking about personal inferiority or superiority.

INDICATORS OF AN INFERIORITY-SUPERIORITY IMBALANCE

Keep in mind that each of us is prone to struggling with the problem of inferiority. But we differ in the way we manifest this difficulty. Some of these manifestations are obvious, others quite subtle.

AN OVERLY APOLOGETIC NATURE

Not a day can go by without each of us making some sort of error. Although our goal is to become conformed to the image of Christ, in humility we must admit a tendency toward flawed living that will not be removed until the day we enter heaven. This reality is not pleasant, but it does not mean we should compare ourselves to others unfavorably. We are all "in the same boat," which is to say that we all have the sin nature within. No one should obsess about his being inferior to another.

In spite of the fact that all persons share in having a sin nature within, many individuals have developed a tendency to be so apologetic about their error-prone ways that they separate themselves from others with harsh self-thoughts. They have not learned that though we are inferior to God's perfect standard, we cannot rightly declare one human as inferior to another. These people focus so exclusively on their own weaknesses that they overlook the fact that others have weaknesses too. Consequently, they feel an excessive need to apologize for wrongs.

Keep in mind that an apologetic nature is necessary and good. Repeatedly Scripture instructs us to confess our sins with a spirit of repentance. We would be irresponsible if we never admitted wrongs. The overly apologetic person, however, goes beyond normal repentance in an all-out effort to excuse self's humanness. He has the unrealistic assumption that no one should make mistakes or have weaknesses.

This extreme tendency has its roots in a developmental background that encouraged an overly conscientious nature. Typically, these persons recall times when the reprimands they received focused on the ideal that was missed. What was communicated to them was not constructive but instead served to highlight failure. Additionally, when their behavior was good, extreme emphasis was given to the fact that it should always be that good. A boy might be told, "You handled that situation well. Why can't you act like this more often?"

The overly apologetic person is so concerned with correctly fitting the mold that he is vigilant to avoid any hint of missing the mark. The apologies he habitually gives are not true statements of remorse for genuine misdeeds, however. Rather, they are subtle pleas to be spared the condemnation that is "supposed to" accompany a revelation of humanness.

A BLINDNESS TO OTHERS' SIMILAR FLAWS

Once a married couple told me how awful they felt about themselves as parents. When I asked them to tell me why they believed they were terrible parents, the description they gave of their home life was like that of any other normal family. Although they had made errors, those errors were similar to the ones all parents make in rearing children. Their feelings of inferiority had been exaggerated by their lack of awareness that they were similar to other people.

Few people can recall background experiences that included honest, constructive conversations about the weaknesses shared by all persons. We have already discussed the fact that many are unfamiliar with the emotions that are at the core of our natures. Likewise, we can assume that few have a good grasp of the basics of sinful human nature. And because most of us are too embarrassed to ask parents and teachers questions about our inner struggles, we are likely to carry erroneous assumptions about ourselves for years. As long as we feel we are nursing secret sins shared by no one else, we suffer emotionally.

Probably the most clear-cut example of this problem lies in the discomfort we feel over our sexual lusts. It is true that every human being has unsavory sexual thoughts that *should* produce shame and humility, which in turn should lead to a willingness to yield the area of sexuality to God. Anyone who proclaims lust to be wholesome is unfamiliar with or unconcerned about God's beautiful design of sexual purity within marital boundaries. But the person who declares himself inferior to others because he experiences unwholesome sexual lusts is inaccurately assuming a status of distinction from others. He gives the impression that he is unaware that *all* persons have this problem—all are equal in the need for repentance. When Jesus declared lust to be on par with adultery (Matthew 5:27-28), He drew attention to the fact that no one could pound his chest in moral pride. Within each person are dark thoughts known only to God.

This same truth could be applied to a myriad of other secret sins. For example, in the passage just mentioned Jesus declared that even though most of us will never murder, we all have an inner disposition to hate. Likewise, every person is susceptible to envy, selfishness, control tactics, impatience, and the like. Individuals vary in the frequency and intensity of those problems, but all persons are in need of salvation—we are inferior to God's perfection but not to one another.

Because of our guilt, we prefer to hide discomforting facts from one another. Consequently, each person is painfully aware of his own weaknesses but relatively unaware of the weaknesses of others. When the sins of others thus remain unknown, it is common to presume that self is worse than others. The possibility of this happening increases when the basic needs have been insufficiently addressed.

AN INABILITY TO ADMIT WEAKNESSES

Everything we say and do is a commentary of our foundational feelings of security. Paradoxically, persons who can admit weaknesses illustrate a type of secure strength, whereas those who attempt to appear forever strong are demonstrating an inward weakness.

It is a fact that each individual has insecurities and inadequacies. But because of competitiveness, many seem to thrive on the false notion that they should rise above the crowd by exhibiting no flaws. Presumably this would "prove" one's superiority. But in truth, this effort only proves that the individual is not willing to be identified as mortal. His desire to be beyond weaknesses indicates a lack of genuine self-acceptance. His ego is so fragile that it cannot admit the truth. He needs to coddle himself with flattery.

The inability to admit weaknesses can be traced to Adam and Eve's original sin. When Satan enticed them to become so self-preoccupied that they attempted to be as God, the couple immediately recognized this sin, but instead of openly admitting it, they attempted to hide. Then when they were "found" by God, their next tactic was to shift blame. This tendency has continued through successive generations to the present. Each child has learned to follow the pattern of refusing to admit weaknesses.

Only when the five basic needs are successfully addressed can a developing individual come naturally to show a willingness to be open about his inadequacies. But if he lacks fulfillment of one or more of these needs, the tendency to be defensive increases. For example, when love or freedom is missing, it is risky for the individual to be open with others because he has not been encouraged to develop an authentic self. Phoniness becomes habitual for him, followed by a hidden feeling of uneasiness about what really lies within.

Jesus once stated, "Whoever shall deny Me before men, I will also deny him before My Father" (Matthew 10:33). In essence, Jesus was declaring that we each have a need to declare our inadequacies, thus to call on Him to save us. If we refuse openly to profess a need for Him, we lose in two respects: we do not receive His empowerment, and we are left with the inadequacy we wish to deny.

A NEED TO CONTROL

The vast majority of people who struggle with inferiority are not content to merely "sit and take it." They desire to "get even" in some fashion. They attempt to get even by adopting controlling behaviors. Gaining control creates an illusion of compensation that temporarily eases inadequate feelings. It gives a temporary feeling of smugness that offsets one's feeling of inadequacy. Unfortunately it also leads to further frustration, since controlling behavior usually creates a never ending cycle of competition.

The control tactics used by insecure persons are widely varied. Some individuals attempt to take charge through direct means. They are bossy, opinionated, abrasive, or critical. Such behavior gives them an immediate sense of self-importance, even though it comes with the price of relational discomfort. Others are more subtle. They silently withdraw, or they are evasive, stubborn, or noncompliant. Although such behavior may not attract excessive attention, it serves the purpose of "evening the score" when the individual is on the deficit end of a relationship.

Often control tactics are not consciously enacted. Most persons do not specifically plan to use controlling behaviors as a means of responding to feelings of inferiority. They are probably not even aware that their need for control indicates the presence of a struggle with inferiority. It is likely that they have not considered the fact that Satan's original temptation to become like God was intended to create in man a craving for control. This lack of awareness causes the problem to continue unabated. Unwittingly, persons who respond to the tension of inferiority by becoming controlling are doing what comes naturally to all of us as sinners.

Unfortunately, control tactics do not produce lasting benefits. Consider the process: a person feels inferior and compensates by adopting control maneuvers, inevitably communicating from a false base of superiority; in turn, the person he is trying to control and thus push into a position of inferiority fails to appreciate the designation and responds by control tactics of his own, thus keeping in motion a seesaw game of "one up, one down."

A man who was belittled in his childhood may in adulthood respond by dominating his wife and children. The wife and children react against him with anger and noncompliance. Or perhaps a woman was once pushed to excel, thus creating in her a sense of insecurity every time she made a mistake. She reacts to this insecurity by becoming bossy, but in doing so creates enemies who think of her as unloving. A teenager who feels he can never please his parents may take out his insecurities by teasing his younger sister, which in turn creates a home atmosphere of constant feuding.

Ultimately, the need to be in control perpetuates rather than alleviates inferiority feelings. The behavior may seem to indicate power, but the thoughts underlying it reflect weakness: "I am afraid my circumstances will get the best of me, so I'd better create my own power base before I'm completely overwhelmed." As long as such notions are dominant in a person's mind, he will continue to experience the tension of inferiority.

REGULAR IRRITABILITY

I am always leery of the salesman who pushes his product with extra vigor. When he goes on and on about how I cannot live without his product, instinctively I begin to wonder, *What is wrong with this item, since it requires such heavy salesmanship?* I suspect that I am not alone in this tendency.

I have the same type of curiosity when an individual is chronically irritable. Irritants arise when persons feel mistreated. The proper expression of annoyance can actually serve the positive function of communicating one's belief in his own dignity. After all, if a person was treated improperly and never felt the slightest irritation, that would be abnormal and even unhealthy. But when an individual expresses irritation at every turn, it indicates an oversensitivity to condescension. Like the salesman who works too hard to push his wares, the regularly irritable person creates an image of himself as one whose "product" is weak and thus needs excessive priming.

The irritated person is communicating: "Hey, I deserve respect, so please don't treat me in a lowly fashion." But irritability is so offensive that the message the person wants to communicate is not registered, thus assuring that his feelings of inadequacy will not be properly resolved. Until he learns to communicate in a way more palatable to others, his underlying feelings of inferiority will persist.

NEEDED: A BIBLICAL VIEW OF COEQUALITY

It has been mentioned that each person is inferior to God's perfect standard. Thus an acknowledgment of our inadequacies is necessary, for it causes us to appeal to God for deliverance. The mistake made by many of us, though, is to assume one person can be proven to be inferior to another person. Thus, we can become unnecessarily bogged down with a sense of inadequacy not intended for us by God.

A biblical character who found balance in his beliefs about his comparative standing with others was the apostle Peter, a man prone to swings of mood. At times Peter felt that he was lower than anyone on earth. At other times he exhibited an arrogance hardly befitting a man of God. The experience that introduced him to the concept of one person's coequal status to another came well into his years of ministry as an evangelist.

Acts 10 relates the story of Peter's encounter with the Roman soldier Cornelius. Prior to his meeting with Cornelius, Peter staunchly believed that the status of the Jews as a chosen people gave them superiority over the Gentiles. But the Holy Spirit instructed Peter to set aside his old notions of superiority and witness to Cornelius. When Cornelius received Peter into his home and told the apostle how God's Spirit had prepared his heart to receive the gospel, Peter declared, "I most certainly understand now that God is not one to show partiality." (v. 34). Peter's experience thus taught him that no human should be designated as either higher or lower than another. God loves each the same.

The implication of this scriptural teaching is broad. Although it does not negate the notion of organizational roles within the church, government, or family, it affirms the concept of the coequality of each person with another. Although individuals possess differing skills, talents, and gifts, no one has greater or lesser value to God.

Any communication of oneself that creates a one-up, one-down atmosphere is not appropriate. Any attitude that leads to a posture of inequity to others is in error. Any behavior that puts other persons down is unbiblical. God does not want us to relate to one another in such a fashion. Consequently, the individual who experiences the tension of inferiority needs to rethink his foundational beliefs about one individual's comparative standing with another. By grasping the concept of God's impartiality, he can develop a new mind-set anchored in the truth of the equality of all persons.

Part 2

Scripture's Answers
Produce Composure

SEVEN

SCRIPTURE'S ANSWERS TO OUR UNMET NEEDS

We have discussed how a past marked by unmet needs can result in a life-style of tension manifested in mental and emotional strain. But we need not surrender in despair. There is good news. God has made the human personality quite resilient. Even when we have been repeatedly exposed to improper input, we can still adjust for the better. God has a knack for taking negative circumstances and working them to our advantage. His Holy Spirit is actively engaged in the business of turning lives plagued by stress into lives distinguished by composure and confidence.

To grow beyond past tensions, God *does* require a willingness to allow Him to create in us a new approach to living. The process of sanctification (growing into His likeness) is a joint venture in which He provides the strength and we provide the mind yielded to His guidance. When we open our minds to ideas different from those taught in imperfect human circumstances, we discover the wealth of God's truth that will literally transform a life once plagued by the maladies of flawed relationships. Romans 12:2 explains, "Do not be conformed to this world, but be transformed by the renewing of your mind." The mind that learns to exchange the false messages of the world for the enlightenment of God's truth becomes stable and calm.

I am acquainted with a forty-year-old man of Chinese ancestry who was born in Hong Kong and now lives in America. He did not immigrate until he was fourteen, when he had already been fully indoctrinated in Chinese language, customs, and education. He experienced a tremendous culture shock when he moved to America that left him in a state of confusion for much of his adolescence. His attempts to master a new language and integrate into a vastly different culture were difficult, and frequently he fumbled in his efforts to "act American." But by his twentieth birthday his new language skills were impressive, and eventually he found his niche in the world of business, becoming financially independent and socially adept.

When I asked this man how he had made such a successful cross-cultural adjustment, he explained that he had to undergo a "thinking transplant." Not only did he have to learn to speak new words but he had to learn to think in new ways. What seemed normal in his old culture had to be set aside as he became acclimated to the standards of the new. At first his efforts felt unnatural, but in time they were habitual. Finally they became instinctive. It was no overnight transformation, and it required years of concentration. But through dogged persistence his efforts paid off.

In a similar way, persons who have a history of unmet needs can undergo a thinking transplant. Adjusting psychological and spiritual ideas may at first seem forced. In fact, it can feel as awkward as speaking in a foreign language. But when we persist in focusing on God's truth and consistently yielding to the Holy Spirit's guidance, change is not only possible but inevitable.

The first part of this book was intended to present the basic needs each person has and to show how unmet needs result in various forms of tension. This identification process is vital, for it helps us focus on areas of personal weakness and vulnerability. It creates in us an awareness of the areas in our lives that most need God's transformation. Once the identification process is well underway, the next step is to incorporate God's ideas as a counter to the erroneous ideas created by unmet needs.

It is difficult to find composure when one's personal history has provided an insufficient foundation for learning

God's ways. In an ideal, sinless environment we would have been given the benefit of *experiential* instruction in God's truth, which would have been the best form of instruction. Yet we can still rejoice because we can substitute learning God's ways on an *intellectual* level, with the intent of *applying* such knowledge in new patterns of living. That is the essence of becoming transformed by the renewing of the mind.

Matthew 5:48 renders the instruction, "Therefore you are to be perfect, as your heavenly Father is perfect." Far from imposing on us the impossible task of total perfection, the context of this verse implies that though we will never achieve perfection, because of indwelling sin, we can determine what are God's ways and consistently aim for His best. In fact, the Greek word translated "perfect" is *teleios*, which means to become complete, or mature. Though our efforts to be transformed will not be complete this side of heaven, our efforts can be consistently progressive. The same concept is echoed in Philippians 1:6: "For I am confident of this very thing, that He who began a good work in you will perfect it until the day of Christ Jesus." With this concept in mind, Paul then wrote, "Forgetting what lies behind and reaching forward to what lies ahead, I press on toward the goal for the prize of the upward call of God in Christ Jesus" (3:13-14). We *can* be transformed, no matter what the past gave us.

READDRESSING THE BASIC NEEDS

Keeping in mind a commitment to exchange old messages for God's truth, we can reexamine the five basic needs to determine how God wants us to think and thus change our present and future ways.

LOVE AND GOD'S ACCEPTANCE

When the Swiss theologian Karl Barth was on a lecture tour of America, he was asked what was the deepest truth that could be known by man. He paused momentarily, then responded, "Jesus loves me this I know, for the Bible tells me so." Indeed, his response went to the core of Christian belief. It is a profound and undeniable truth that we are deeply loved by God, so much so, that in spite of our rebellion against Him, He chooses to seek us out for the purpose of sharing that love with us for eternity.

That is why God created us with the need for love. If we did not have the need, we would have no appreciation of the gift. The need creates in us a desire to be satisfied. It causes us to seek out the source of its fulfillment. So as long as we hunger instinctively for love, we maintain the ability to establish a relationship with the One who is love.

But as I noted, the problem of rejection throws us out of sync and obstructs our effort to feel that we are loved. God's original design designated human relationships as conduits for His love. As love is given and received among family, friends, and acquaintances, individuals are equipped to know His love clearly. But because of sin, many persons have scrapped that plan. The design itself is still perfect, but because of generation after generation of failure to live according to the design, many have lost sight of the permanence of God's love. God's character has never changed, but our interpretation of it has been skewed by experiences of rejection. Consequently, we need to learn to relate to God *separately* from our flawed human relationships.

It is possible to overcome the tension introduced by rejection by determining to become fully acquainted with the truth of His acceptance of us. Whether or not the persons in our lives have loved us unconditionally, whether or not we have actually felt their love, God's love is constant. Ephesians 2:4-5 is clear: "But God, being rich in mercy, because of His great love with which He loved us, even when we were dead in our transgressions, made us alive together with Christ." His love for us has never ceased, though the persons entrusted with the demonstration of that love may have failed. So rather than listening to flawed human messages of rejection, we can go to God's promises and claim the love intended for us all along (fig. 7.1).

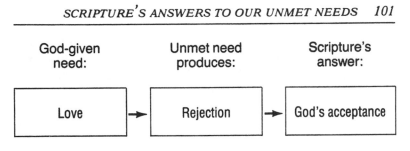

God-given need:	Unmet need produces:	Scripture's answer:
Love →	Rejection →	God's acceptance

Figure 7.1

Many people find the notion of becoming focused on the truth of God's acceptance easier said than done. I am frequently asked, "How do you turn off painful feelings of rejection and respond to the love of God, particularly when it seems so unnatural?" The answer is that no one can turn off emotions like a light switch. Responding to God's acceptance requires a thorough and ongoing examination of the facts and a total willingness to live within the framework of those facts.

First, we can cling to such verses as Romans 5:8: "But God demonstrates His own love toward us, in that while we were yet sinners, Christ died for us." We can draw inspiration from the many stories of Christ's compassion for the hurt. We can know of our value to God by studying His plan to take us home to an eternal life of bliss when we die. Second, we can understand that we were made to resist rejection instinctively. The fact that we become frustrated, sad, or fearful when others mistreat us shows that we have an instinctive belief that we are not to be rebuked but rather to be loved. Knowing such truth, we enter the process of shaping our ideas to conform to that revelation.

Yet most efforts to change break down at this point. Many so wish that their environment would solve their problems that they resist exerting the effort to adjust from the inside out. Rather than saying, "I'm committed to learning and living God's truth," they say, "Why can't my world do what it's supposed to do?"

We can never count on our circumstances to match God's original design. That is why God has made the process of change a personal one. His grace offers us the chance to adjust even when those around us continue in sin. By indoctrinating our minds with His truth, we can detach ourselves from false messages imposed on us by misguided persons. We will then learn to meditate daily on thoughts designed to prevent experiences of rejection from holding power over us. Those thoughts might include the following:

- "Though people have wronged me, I can live in the confidence that I am still valuable to my Creator."
- "God's opinion of me is far more important than others."
- "Jesus' willingness to leave His throne to die for me on the cross indicates the depth of God's desire to relate lovingly with me."
- "If Jesus was willing to befriend those with miserable pasts, I assume that same desire exists in Him as it relates to me."
- "I'll not allow the rejection of me by others to erase my trust in God's acceptance of me."

FREEDOM AND THE PRIVILEGE OF CHOICES

Because God's blueprint for mankind calls for healthy doses of freedom, we thrive when we are allowed balanced self-expression. It is no accident that all peoples of the world prefer the opportunity to live without the constraints of a dictator. God created us free and has no desire to relate to us as robots whose responses are programmed. By giving us a capacity for freedom, He ensured that our behavior and emotions can have purpose and our relationships can have depth. When someone is given permission to choose the course of his behavior, that behavior has meaning that robot-like activity could never match.

Because freedom is such an integral part of God's creative genius, it follows that when freedom is denied, undesirable results follow. In the previous chapters, I observed that a past which featured confinement will contribute to many manifestations of tension. When the human spirit is unduly chained it will be susceptible to unsavory emotions, thoughts, and behavior. Frustration will grow and will poison one's sense of inner well being. As long as freedom is prescribed for us by God, we will have a chance for composure when it is offered, and we will suffer when it is withheld.

When persons examine past experiences of confinement, they usually discover that the confinement they experienced adversely affected their thinking patterns. Typically, they have become so accustomed to being restricted that they learn to approach life with a powerful sense of duty that allows them little freedom to sift through options. Fear and guilt have become the primary motivators for right living, so that even when they do the right thing they feel only a minimal feeling of satisfaction. Eventually, many such individuals become rebellious in their attitude and behavior, a rebellion they express either in open defiance or in quiet resistance.

In order to break the tension caused by confinement, a person who has been confined can find hope in the fact that in spite of the desire other persons have to restrict us, God continues to offer us the privilege of choices. Though man has distorted the operation of free will in our lives, God continually allows us to retain the ability to choose for ourselves what will become of our lives. And as we receive this privilege, we come closer to experiencing the tension-free lives we prefer. When Joshua spoke to the people of Israel about their habits of life, he underscored this privilege: "Choose for yourselves today whom you will serve" (Joshua 24:15). He knew that a coerced devotion to God's ways (or to anyone else's ways, for that matter) is shallow devotion at best. So he put the options before the people in a clear and unmistakable way, knowing that free will was God's preference over confinement (fig. 7.2).

God-given need:	Unmet need produces:	Scripture's answer:

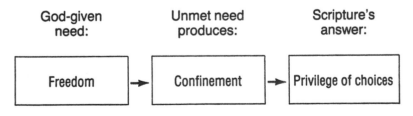

| Freedom | → | Confinement | → | Privilege of choices |

Figure 7.2

The implications of this truth are broad. It means that when we are exposed to an atmosphere that "puts on the clamps," we can know that no matter what is said by others, we *always* have choices. We can choose to allow any number of attitudes to guide us. We can choose to give prominence to negative emotions. We can choose to yield to God's qualities of patience and kindness. We can choose to give up in defeat, or we can choose to live in the victory of salvation. We can choose to bear grudges, or we can choose to forgive. We can choose to confront wrongs openly, or we can choose to accept negative circumstances. We can choose to ignore God, or we can choose to be consumed with awareness of Him. Although external options are frequently limited, we *always* have a wide array of internal options. By acknowledging the privilege of choices, we discover that we are not doomed to be controlled completely by other people and circumstances of our lives. We can shift responsibility for our lives away from others and take it upon ourselves.

Claiming the privilege of choices is particularly difficult for individuals who have been exposed to the more extreme forms of confinement. Those who have been harshly regulated and manipulated are more likely to desire revenge or at least fair judgment. They see anything short of severe retribution as allowing controlling people to get away with destructive behavior. Yet in spite of the legitimacy of their cries for revenge, controlled individuals must learn to focus on how they will choose to respond, rather than focusing on how others should respond. It will help them if they admit (however reluctantly) that those who have acted harshly are also free people. They have elected to use their God-given free will destructively, but that is their prerogative. Eventually they will answer to God for their actions. But just because they have mishandled a God-given gift of freedom, that does not mean that we are compelled to match their poor judgment with bad choices of our own. Rather than becoming like them with respect to bitterness or inappropriate behavior, we can choose to be released from tension by opting for God's ways.

When we acknowledge the privilege of choices, our emotions and actions are guided by rational thoughts:

- "No circumstance has ultimate power over me unless I allow it."
- "All options are available to me—both sinful and godly—and if I am to become a composed person, I will freely select the godly."
- "My responses to the past are ultimately my own responsibility. At some point in life I become accountable before God for who I am."
- "It is the prerogative of others to behave in dictatorial ways, and it is my prerogative to determine how I will respond."
- "God wants my life to have meaning, and I am responding to His desire when I freely determine the ideas and philosophies I will follow."

INTERNAL CONTROLS AND THE GIFT OF STRENGTH

By offering freedom, God has shown that He does not want our motivation for living to be externally determined. He prefers that we grapple inwardly with the beliefs that ultimately will guide us. Thus He created in us a need for an internal system of control. Whether we realize it or not, by the adult years each person has developed a sustaining philosophy of life. Typically, those who suffer from tension either have committed themselves to a system of inner controls that is unscriptural, or they have suffered from the lack of true depth in the beliefs that guide them. In the latter case, they have such weak internal controls that they fluctuate easily with the circumstances of the moment.

But our Lord is gracious. When we have lived within an environment that did not teach us properly to meet the need for inner control, He Himself becomes an enabler who provides the inner strength necessary to live within a controlled philosophy. One of the functions of His Holy Spirit is to provide the guidance and empowerment for living. This means that when individuals are lacking in internal controls, they can draw upon Him for this strength. Second Timothy 1:7 speaks of this: "For God has not given us a spirit of timidity, but of power and love and discipline." Psalms 28:7 also testifies, "The Lord is my strength and my shield; my heart trusts in Him, and I am helped." In spite of a background that might have denied the development of well-conceived internal controls, it is never too late to search out the Lord for His empowerment. This is the solution for a life hindered by a lack of true inner discipline (fig. 7.3).

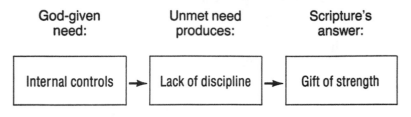

God-given need:	Unmet need produces:	Scripture's answer:
Internal controls ➞	Lack of discipline ➞	Gift of strength

Figure 7.3

In the book *Fearfully and Wonderfully Made*, Paul Brand and Philip Yancey make a point through an analogy taken from human physiology. They compare the skeletal structure of a human to that of a crustacean (i.e., a lobster or a crayfish) and extol the superiority of the human skeleton, because its bones are internal rather than external. Bones give human beings their shape and mobility. An internal bone structure allows for greater flexibility and unrestrained growth whereas an external bone structure causes the creature to be rigid and have little room for growth. Brand and Yancey then explain that "Jesus never described anything representing an exoskeleton which would define all Christians. He kept pointing to higher, more lofty demands, using words like love and joy and fullness of life—internal words."[1] We need to be guided by well thought-out concepts rather than by conformity simply for conformity's sake.

Individuals whose past did not provide the environment for developing internal controls can find hope in the fact that it is never too late to contemplate one's guiding philosophy. By determining to dig for answers to essential questions, a person can develop internal controls. It will not be an over-

1. Paul Brand and Philip Yancey, *Fearfully and Wonderfully Made* (Grand Rapids: Zondervan, 1980), p. 109.

night process, but it can be accomplished by anyone willing to think. A person can meditate upon Scripture, he can use prayer as a means of finding God's will, he can study books, he can attend seminars. The growing person will learn to think not in terms of what someone else's opinion is, but instead to think in terms of opinions he has discovered on his own. When the source for this inner sense of control is the Word of God, he can be assured of an inner strength that supersedes worldly tension.

When God's strength is found through internal controls, certain guiding thoughts will become predominant:

- "The Lord's strength is readily available because it is within my mind, guided by the Holy Spirit."
- "Even though others question me, I know who I am and will therefore persevere."
- "The ideas that guide me can be trusted because I have found them in God's Word and have made them my own."
- "Past traumas will not haunt me because I have learned how to grow from them."
- "My relationship with God is not formal religion but true spirituality, and as a result my spirit is at peace."

EMOTIONAL FAMILIARITY AND RICHNESS OF EXPERIENCE

Imagine feasting on your favorite meal, soaking in the aroma and savoring each flavorful bite. Personally, I am a soft touch for barbecue. My idea of a relaxed summer afternoon includes time hovering over the backyard grill, slowly nursing specially spiced meats, salivating as the lazy smoke sends up a smell that primes me for the moment we all get to sit down and "dig in." If I had no ability to smell or to taste, such an activity would mean little to me. Eating would merely be the mechanical function of supplying my stomach with nutrients to keep my body performing. Meals would be a gray experience.

That is the way life can be for those who do not have the ability to balance their emotions properly. When a person's background has not given him true familiarity with his emotions, he loses richness of experience. When I speak of becoming familiar with one's emotions, I mean more than merely developing the capacity to express emotions outwardly, though that is certainly part of it. Emotional familiarity—emotional competence—includes understanding the purpose of one's feelings and comprehending how they fit into God's plan for a Spirit-led life-style. It means that one has insight into the harmful emotions of aggressive anger, false guilt, or insecure fear, an insight that thereby leads to taking the proper steps for yielding negative emotions to God. And it also means having an awareness of the way the upbeat emotions —joy and love and contentment, to name a few—can enhance relational skills and personal fulfillment. When an individual is deficient in emotional competence, sin makes him prone to experiencing undesirable emotions often, thus dampening his entire life experience.

Yet even though a familiarity with emotions may not be first nature, any individual who chooses to confront this unmet need can make significant progress in finding rich experiences in balanced emotions. Without question, the book of Psalms is the most emotional of Scripture. In Psalm 145:8 the subjective nature of God is described: "The Lord is gracious and merciful; slow to anger and great in lovingkindness." Then Psalm 147:1 encourages our subjective response to Him: "Praise the Lord! For it is good to sing praises to our God; for it is pleasant and praise is becoming." God wants us to be familiar with our emotions in order to bring a depth to our lives that would otherwise be circumscribed by sin. This emotional experience can be an integral part of our relationship with Him and of our relations with family and friends (fig. 7.4).

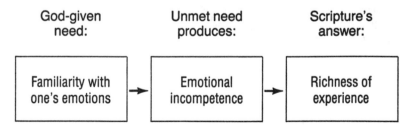

God-given need:	Unmet need produces:	Scripture's answer:
Familiarity with one's emotions	Emotional incompetence	Richness of experience

Figure 7.4

Often persons with a history of unbalanced emotions will report that they cannot imagine themselves experiencing emotional richness. On the one extreme, individuals prone to worry or impatience or depression are likely to assume that their tendency to feel bothersome emotions is a habit they cannot overcome. On the other extreme, people who are prone to repress their emotions, or to express them only reservedly, feel awkward in expressing their emotions openly. In either case, the word *can't* is actually an escape. *Won't* would be the more appropriate term. Because we have been created by God to find fullness of life through emotions, we can be assured that He will enable us to experience balance. Once we acknowledge the possibility of being familiar with our emotions, we can shift our thoughts from "Can I do it?" to "How will it happen?"

Many persons will find Christian counseling necessary if they are to come to terms with their emotions. They will find it helpful to read Christian books that give insight into ways of gaining emotional balance and learning how to communicate themselves to others effectively. They can hold frank discussion with family members, who can offer them constructive suggestions for bringing depth to relationships. Although at first the adjustments they make may feel unnatural, eventually the adjustments will become integral to their character. In time, their behavior will be guided by a new way of thinking:

- "I want to become adept in loving relationships because that is what constitutes real success."
- "Expressing my emotions appropriately is something I *can* do with God's help."
- "Knowing how emotions are related to my spirituality is important to me."
- "I would like to encourage others to be open with me regarding their feelings and perceptions."
- "When I am interacting with others, I will attempt to look beyond the facts and into the feelings beneath the behavior."

No subject known to man is more in need of contemplation than the character of God. Because any explanation of life's meaning begins and ends with Him, we lack wholeness if our minds only infrequently focus on who He is and what He requires of us. God has created in each person a "God vacuum"—a yearning to relate to the Ultimate One. If this yearning is not fulfilled, a feeling of emptiness results; if it is successfully pursued, a sense of completeness comes about. Romans 1:19 explains that even the unrighteous foes of God have an indwelling understanding of His existence: "That which is known about God is evident within them; for God made it evident to them." The task of each person is to reach a personal understanding of God, culminating in a life's commitment to Him.

Two categories of people suffer tension because this need for God is unmet: those who have been reared with little or no motivation to know God and those who have been taught many facts about God but have never been prompted to contemplate Him on a deep level. Modern churches are full of individuals in the latter group. Inevitably, both they and the persons who have little knowledge of God will suffer tension, because they do not have the full range of skills to respond to the strains of sin.

Fortunately, a history lacking in deep contemplation of God can be remedied by putting life into an eternal perspective. One can begin to do that by realizing that the true substance of existence is not material but spiritual. For example, most of us have concluded that the things which truly satisfy cannot be touched or measured: love, laughter, empathy, respect, kindness, humility. And virtually all agree that in spite of the difficulty of explaining the origin of the earth and of mankind, earth and mankind had to begin with a decision by Someone, even if that Someone is too complicated for our minds to grasp. It is pure foolishness to deny this. Most people understand that there is life after our days on earth are complete—there is an Existence much grander than we now know. The apostle Paul, who himself had to learn a new way of thinking about God, encouraged his readers to draw close to God by considering His grandeur, and in doing so finding an eternal perspective that would outlast anything on earth: "Oh, the depth of the riches both of the wisdom and knowledge of God! How unsearchable are His judgments and unfathomable His ways!" (Romans 11:33). He knew that the contemplation of such a Subject is the remedy for the tension of spiritual immaturity (fig. 7.5).

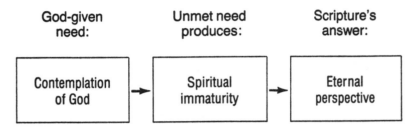

God-given need:	Unmet need produces:	Scripture's answer:
Contemplation of God	Spiritual immaturity	Eternal perspective

Figure 7.5

By gaining a whole perspective of God and our relationship to Him, our tensions from the past can be interpreted through that new perspective. We can derive hope from the truth that though God abhors sin, and though He allows sin to run its course, He has made it possible for us to be delivered from it. We can learn to give Him our devotion, knowing how risky it is to depend upon worldly circumstances for contentment. We give Him our devotion in several stages. First, we commit ourselves to allowing Jesus Christ to be Master of our eternal destiny, claiming Him as the substitutionary payment for our sins. Next, we adopt daily a willingness to consult Him through prayer and Bible study, so that we can learn His thoughts and thereby allow Him to lead the way in our lives. Concentration on this effort is paramount.

When this new way of doing things is applied consistently, a new confidence will appear inwardly, a supernatural capacity for kindness and patience will grow, and God's thoughts will become natural to us:

- "If I am to find peace, I must consult the Author of all peace."
- "Though the past has given me many problems, my future is secure because Christ is my enabler now and in heaven."
- "I may not always understand suffering, but I know God is watching over me and will never let me suffer beyond what I can handle."
- "There is never a problem without an ultimate solution."
- "Meditating on God's ways creates perspective in pressing times."

SUMMARY

Romans 8:28 praises God's willingness to carry us through problems created by sin. No matter how negative our experiences have been, our unmet needs can be resolved when we seek out God's message of redemption: "We know that God causes all things to work together for good to those who love God, to those who are called according to His purposes." We *can* find solutions for each of our unmet needs (fig. 7.6).

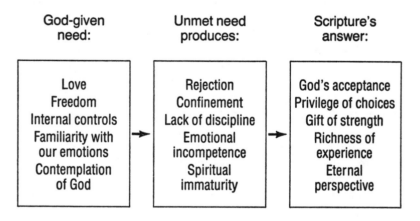

God-given need:	Unmet need produces:	Scripture's answer:
Love Freedom Internal controls Familiarity with our emotions Contemplation of God	Rejection Confinement Lack of discipline Emotional incompetence Spiritual immaturity	God's acceptance Privilege of choices Gift of strength Richness of experience Eternal perspective

Figure 7.6

Just as unmet needs produce tension in varying manifestations, the resolution of those needs leads to composure. And that composure is manifested in ways that counteract the tensions of the past: (1) the mind of distress can be replaced by an overcomer's mind-set, (2) the root of bitterness can be supplanted by a willingness to yield to God's sovereignty, (3) unresolved guilt can be exchanged for the grace of God, (4) dependence-independence imbalances can be stabilized by a biblical foundation of stability, and (5) inferiority-superiority struggles can be checked by setting aside unnecessary competitiveness. The concluding chapters of this book will explore these five manifestations of the resolution of our unmet needs.

EIGHT

THE OVERCOMER'S MIND-SET

A special class of individuals distinguishes itself by a refusal to be held down by negative circumstances. The people in this class are determined to grow in spite of adversity; they are not martyrs or nail-tough stoics. They are realists who have willfully chosen to make responsible decisions even though they have been exposed to unfair circumstances and unwarranted difficulties. They are overcomers. Overcomers are not easily categorized, for among them are educated and uneducated people, white collar and blue collar workers, the young, the old, extroverts, introverts, homemakers, working mothers, the sophisticated, and the unsophisticated. The single trait that binds them together is what might be called "positive stubbornness."

In earlier chapters we discussed the importance of the mind-set—the filter that screens each emotion, behavior, and communication. We noted that persons who have not come to terms with their unmet needs are likely to develop a mind of distress, typified by the "victim" and the "defeatist." But they do not have to develop such a mind-set. They can develop the mind-set of the overcomer (fig. 8.1). That mind-set is a natural by-product of efforts scripturally to confront personal areas of need.

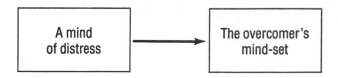

Figure 8.1

An overcomer is defined as one who does not sink to and remain in defeat when he is under personal siege. Instead, he sets his mind on the Word of God and yields his spirit to the victorious Holy Spirit. Resolved needs can feed into the mind-set of "overcoming."

Acceptance by God gives an individual the sense of belonging. Though he may have felt the pain of being unloved by significant others, he has the ability to see through the sinfulness that lies behind rejection. He knows that the God of all creation declares him valuable, and is guided by the thought *If God is for us who will be against us?*

The privilege of choices reminds us that although we may be chained in various forms of external confinement, we do not have to concede ultimate defeat. Other people may control many elements of our environment, but the direction of our mind can still be guided by free will, an element no one can take from us. Once we have made the decision to choose consistently to follow God's ways over man's ways, we will have decided as well to give no one power over our lives that actually belongs to God.

The gift of strength empowers suffering persons with the supernatural ability to rise above adversity. These individuals are aware that they themselves do not have the full measure of strength to fend off the discouraging consequences of mistreatment. But because they have disciplined themselves to yield to the Holy Spirit's guidance, their thoughts take on a confident perspective.

Richness in experiences causes people who have suffered to know that in spite of past difficulties, a fullness of life still exists and can bring them joy and contentment. As they become familiar with the negative and positive emotions, and as they learn to become balanced in their emotions, their thoughts are strengthened by the experience of contentment that accompanies subjective balance.

Eternal perspective reminds an individual that no matter what he experiences in the world, God is much greater. God assures that ultimately there will be victory over sin and suffering. A person who keeps this truth in mind will not let his thoughts be so grounded in temporal matters that the present world is all that is known to them. He focuses his thoughts on the things that are above, and his whole personality learns to filter matters through God's perspective.

When the mind has been transformed by Scripture's answers, the tension of unmet needs can be replaced by the mind-set of an overcomer (fig. 8.2).

Unmet need produces:	Scripture's answer:	Results in:
Rejection Confinement Lack of discipline Emotional incompetence Spiritual immaturity	God's acceptance Privilege of choices Gift of strength Richness of experience Eternal perspective	The overcomer's mind-set

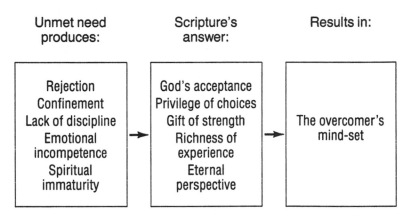

Figure 8.2

THE BELIEFS OF AN OVERCOMER

Once individuals determine to allow Scripture to show the way to the overcomer's mind-set, they acquire a belief system far different from the ideas found in the mind of distress. Three of the most prominent of these beliefs are discussed here.

BELIEF 1: GOD IS IN CONTROL

This first belief could easily fall into the category of "pat answers," but I do not intend it as such. Ever since Satan's original temptation of Eve, we humans have been vying for control over our own destinies. In spite of being told to stay away from The Tree of the Knowledge of Good and Evil, Adam and Eve determined that they were qualified to assume the position of God, thus making the dreadful decision to take control of their lives. Adam and Eve's desire for control was the beginning of the spiritual and emotional struggles mankind has experienced ever since, and it is the essence of man's sinful nature. When a desire for control is allowed to run rampant, it creates an inability to accept reality and leads people to fantasize about what might have been.

Inevitably, when individuals suffer from painful experiences in the past (especially if their suffering was unmerited), the question arises, "What is God doing? Why is He allowing such pain?" Then, wishing to be in control of events, people add, "I'm certain that if I were God I would not have allowed such problems!" The emotion is understandable, but the desire to second-guess God is dangerous.

Volumes have been written in an attempt to explain human suffering. But truthfully, when we ourselves are the ones who have suffered, all explanations seem insufficient. Though it may be logical to assume that sinful mankind deserves to suffer the consequences of defying God's commandments, our ability to think logically about suffering breaks down when the concept is individualized. That is because we have a hunger for control.

In making peace with problems from the past, overcomers will begin with one assumption above all others: God knows what He is doing. Although the overcomer may not comprehend all there is to know about God, he willingly ascribes total perfection to the One who is beyond error.

The end result of acknowledging God's control is trust. Although the trusting individual may not know all the facts about the One he trusts, he willingly relinquishes control. He believes in the integrity of God's character, with the result that he has confident expectation that God will be the all-loving Provider the Bible says He is. According to Proverbs 3:5-6, when we trust in the Lord with all our hearts, not relying on our own understanding but acknowledging Him, He will direct our paths.

BELIEF 2: ALL PROBLEMS CAN BE RESOLVED IN SOME MANNER

First Corinthians 10:13 promises, "No temptation [tribulation] has overtaken you but such as is common to man; and God is faithful, who will not allow you to be tempted beyond what you are able, but with the temptation will provide the way of escape also, that you may be able to endure it." The key phrase in this verse is the expression "God is faithful." If we have encountered hardships, we can assume that God knows we can handle them. He does not allow us to experience trials he knows are too overpowering for us.

God is not bound by time. Yesterday is just as current to Him as today. And tomorrow is just as familiar to Him as today. In a sense, He stands outside of time, observing all events as if they were all equally in the present. He sees just as clearly what is in our past as He sees what is in our present. He sees what is in our future as if it were in the present. There is nothing in the past, the present, or the future of which He is unaware. He understands how all events are woven together and how they will affect each of us. He is aware of the troublesome events that will cause us irrevocable harm. And He is aware of the troublesome events that may harm but can lead to deep growth. No event escapes His attention.

When God, who is outside time, observes an event or circumstance that is so negative it will cause us irreparable damage, we can be assured that He steers our life's progression in such a way that we will not experience something that cannot be resolved. Though He has set the law of consequence for sin into motion, God's mercy will not allow His created ones to suffer beyond their capacity. His love for us will not permit unbearable pain. It may seem that we have been allowed to suffer unbearable misery, but the God who stands outside time has foreseen the event and has predetermined that indeed we can find resolution and even personal growth. He *will not* allow us to suffer beyond our capacity to cope.

Those who have developed the overcomer's mind-set have given themselves over to the protective care of God. Trusting Him to provide the way out of struggles, they hold firmly to the promise of His complete involvement in their fight against the consequences of sin. Although they are not always "in the know" concerning the resolution God will bring about, they exercise patience, knowing that He will provide them all the support they need.

BELIEF 3: OVERCOMING COMES ONLY IN MANAGEABLE INCREMENTS OF TIME

How many people do you know who are experts at intellectualizing about God's ways but failures at practicing those same truths? Each of us has had the experience of being an expert at applying excellent theories to the problems of others at the same time we are having difficulty in implementing those theories in our own lives.

Overcomers have learned not to fall into the trap of broad theorizing that proves useless in moments of real crises. They are practical enough to think specifically about the ways their beliefs can be applied to difficulties. And they have learned that it is sometimes necessary to implement God's answers in brief increments of time. For example, rather than expounding on broad concepts regarding fifteen reasons worry might gain a foothold in their particular temperament, they establish specific goals to implement in one particular afternoon as ways of keeping their minds from worry. Although they know theories, they are pragmatic and live in the "here and now."

Overcomers are aware that God specifically provides for our immediate needs. Certainly, He has a long-range outlook, but He wants to relate to us in today's terms. For example, during the years the Israelites roamed in the wilderness awaiting entrance into Canaan, God gave them one day's supply of manna each day. When Jesus Christ invited men to follow Him, He told each person to pick up his cross daily. God knows that laziness can befall us when we think we've got it made. He wants a renewal of commitment each day.

Practical living means that an individual who has harbored bitterness will go beyond merely conceptualizing forgiveness. He will develop a daily—sometimes hourly—commitment to the practice of forgiveness. The individual who is prone to feelings of inferiority can claim God's strength just before he interacts with a person who easily evokes negative feelings in him. Because they are time-specific in the overcoming of turmoil from the past, overcomers know that God's victories are concrete and real.

THE PHILIPPIANS 4 PHILOSOPHY

Once an individual's mind is guided by solid beliefs, a consistent philosophy of life takes form, which leads in turn to his making adjustments in life-style habits. As a person's life gains depth and purpose, many of his worries and frivolities fall away. That does not mean that he becomes a sober, serious-minded stick-in-the-mud. Rather, it means that he has escaped the shallowness and futility of a life filled with tension.

One person who developed the overcomer's mind-set—and thus a rewarding life-style—was the apostle Paul. When he was confined in a Roman jail, he wrote a letter to the Philippians telling them how he had learned to live victoriously in spite of his many troubles. Often called the Epistle of Joy, the letter to the Philippians refers to the joys of prayer, of preaching, of faith, of suffering for Christ, of good news from loved ones, of Christian hospitality, of being in the Lord, of the soul winner, and of Christian concern. Most men imprisoned in a dampened cell would have agonized over their ill fortune, but Paul wrote of the things that made him happy. He had discovered that with Christ's indwelling presence, he could live as a man at peace in a turbulent world.

The skeptic might disclaim Paul's attitude, saying, "Paul could have joy because he had a type of relationship with God I can't come close to having." Or he might say, "The suffering I've had is different from the suffering Paul experienced, so the same principles wouldn't necessarily hold true in my case." But such disclaimers merely sidestep one's personal responsibility to embrace the truths taught in God's Word. Paul was an ordinary human being—he had the same feelings as everyone else. His ability to live as an overcomer lay in his willingness to submit totally to God's authority. He knew that anything short of total submission would bring personal disaster.

The fourth chapter of Philippians is the climax of this victorious letter. We can glean specific instructions from it for living with a contentment that transcends circumstances. Listed below are four instructions from this great chapter.

1. BECOME DEEPLY INVOLVED IN A PRAYER LIFE

"Be anxious for nothing, but in everything by prayer and supplication with thanksgiving let your requests be made known to God" (Philippians 4:6).

Imagine a parent who claims to love his child dearly. One day the child has feelings of sadness and shares his needs with his parent. No loving parent would respond to the child by saying, "Get out of here. Your needs mean nothing to me!" The loving parent would be receptive and concerned, making absolutely certain the child knows he can come forward with the most personal of requests. Our heavenly Father has that same desire, but on a far greater scale than any human parent. When a child of His suffers ill treatment, the craving of His heart is to communicate His love. But that cannot be accomplished if we are unwilling to share our needs openly with Him. That is why we are instructed to make our requests known to Him.

Prayer includes the expression of our needs to God, yet it involves so much more than merely repeating petitions. Prayer is the sharing of one's spirit with God. Prayer includes confession of dependency on Him. It involves praise, worship, and searching for His ways. And, interestingly, as Paul introduced the instruction to pray, he used the phrase "be anxious for nothing," indicating that prayer is to be conducted without selfish concerns or fretting. The central purpose of prayer is to create and maintain fellowship with the Father.

I have known many people who have given up on prayer because God did not seem responsive. One woman told me that she had prayed for years for the removal of bitterness in her heart, but it had produced no results. Another stated that repeatedly she had sought forgiveness for past sins, but experienced no feeling of cleansing. In such cases I am inclined to believe that prayer did not actually occur. Demands may have been made of God, or requests may have been recited without there being any belief that they would be granted, but there was no real effort truly to commune with God. When such feeble or misguided attempts at prayer are made, they actually fuel a feeling of tension.

Think about the many ingredients necessary for formulating and maintaining a close friendship. The expression of perspectives, feelings, and interests is necessary. Listening attentively to the friend is also required. Gradually, friends gain a knowledge of one another's unique qualities. Compliments are given. Joy is openly shared—as are struggles. We would have few true friendships if we merely requested favors without also exchanging the elements that bring depth to the relationship.

If human friendships require many components in order to make them real, the same can be said of our relationship with God. With the instruction to commune with Him in prayer is the implication that we must learn to relate to Him beyond superficial levels. We need to involve Him in our needs by exposing our souls to Him, seeking out His will, and becoming aware of His overwhelming concern. We can thus find strength in Him when we verbalize our awareness of his watchful care over us.

2. CONCENTRATE ON THE GOOD THINGS YOU HAVE EXPERIENCED

"Whatever is true, whatever is honorable, whatever is right, whatever is pure, whatever is lovely, whatever is of good repute, if there is any excellence and if anything is worthy of praise, let your mind dwell on these things" (Philippians 4:8).

When an individual comes under oppressive circumstances, his mind tends to be so clouded by overwhelmingly negative feelings that he loses perspective of the good things in life. Often, when a person has been inflicted by unusually negative circumstances, the negative effects can last for years. An individual who has experienced painful rejection will never be able to forget completely the awfulness of his experience. Similarly, an adult who has experienced years of manipulation or torment in a marriage cannot easily blot those memories from his mind. It is normal for him to have thoughts and emotions of a negative nature.

It is painful to carry memories of bad experiences. But one thing is even worse: clinging to painful memories so strongly that the personality acquires the traits disliked in those who inflicted pain. Abused and rejected individuals can harbor negative thoughts for such a long time that they themselves become abusing and rejecting. They may become externally abusive by turning their thoughts against others, or they become internally abusive by turning their thoughts against themselves.

In Philippians 4:8 Paul tells us that when we have received ill treatment, we must guard against letting the experience pollute our thoughts. Keeping in mind the many acts of violence Paul endured, we can assume that he maintained his sanity by remembering that in spite of all the evil he had encountered, some good things were still left. He could recall friends who had shown loyalty when he was publicly scorned. He had memories of the successes God had given him. He knew that in spite of the hateful people he encountered, there were those who loved him. Though Paul was unable to control the external circumstances of his life, with God's strength he could control the direction of his thoughts.

In suggesting that we saturate our minds with thoughts that are pure, Paul was not encouraging denial. The object of his instruction was not intended to produce an "ostrich approach" to problems. Rather, it was intended to emphasize that we can choose for ourselves what traits our personalities will nurture rather than allowing our inner traits to be dictated by others.

3. BE WILLING TO RECEIVE THE CONCERN OF OTHERS

"I have rejoiced in the Lord greatly, that now at last you have revived your concern for me; indeed, you were concerned before, but you lacked opportunity. . . . Nevertheless, you have done well to share with me in my affliction" (Philippians 4:10, 14).

When a friend is in need, most persons are willing to go the extra mile to help him meet his physical and personal needs. But when we are the ones receiving the help, it feels awkward to be showered with kindness. We feel uncomfortable because our situation forces us to acknowledge weakness. And most of us are not predisposed to such self-exposure. Yet part of Paul's ability to maintain calm lay in the encouragement and gifts he received from his friends.

Several years ago I learned how difficult it can be to receive another's help graciously. Both of my legs had been broken in an accident, and I had to endure several surgeries to repair the damage. For a year it was difficult for me to carry out many routine tasks around the house. Being an achiever all my life, I hated to admit inabilities, but in this case they were so obvious I could not hide them. Several men from my church graciously offered their services to me and my family. We had just purchased a new home, and I had been forced to scrap plans for personally installing a new yard. My friends from church voluntarily planted the yard, complete with trees and shrubs, and maintained it weekly. For as long as I was unable to help myself, they insisted that I allow them the pleasure of being kind to me. Yet as much as I appreciated their gesture, I fought the idea that I was in the position of needing help.

When we are encumbered by difficulties, often the most agonizing admission is, "I need help." Proud people that we are, we like to assume we can handle our problems with no outside intervention. We do not relish the prospect of appearing weak. That is especially true when our traumas have embarrassing features and when our pains have uncomfortable emotional roots. Because of the tendency we have not to admit weakness, we are prone to projecting a false image of well-being, which only deepens our inner affliction. The net result can be withdrawal, phoniness, bitterness, and depression.

It is true that we must be tactful when we disclose our neediness, for not all persons will respond to our admission constructively. But we must avoid the extreme of suffering in silence. God desires Christians to be open with each other in sharing needs so that His love can be made manifest. Proverbs 15:22 states, "Without consultation, plans are frustrated." It is impossible to be truly composed and to exchange real love with others when no one is willing to become vulnerable. Just as Paul allowed his Christian brothers and sisters to minister to him, we too can allow ministering in our lives.

4. MAKE CONTENTMENT A SPIRITUAL MATTER

"For I have learned to be content in whatever circumstances I am. . . . I can do all things through Him who strengthens me" (Philippians 4:11, 13).

Most individuals recognize that contentment by definition involves the spirit of a person and should therefore be gained through intangible means. It is easy to argue that contentment cannot always be found in wealth, popularity, or primary relationships. Intellectually we know this. But a strange thing often happens when individuals suffer unduly: their intellectualizations about the source of contentment go right out the window! Though they can recite warnings against putting too much hope in people or in circumstances, they find themselves desperately bemoaning the fact that worldly events failed them.

Most people learn early in life what comprises good relationships. Virtually every individual knows that the qualities of acceptance and harmony are desirable. And though we may not always have fulfillment in these areas, we look forward to the day when we can have them regularly. Armed with hope and idealism, we yearn for experiences that will give us what we know is God-ordained. Consequently, when we are offered rejection and debasement, that hope is dashed, causing disillusionment and trauma as we are forced to let go of the ideals that once seemed plausible.

When we give up idealistic hope, there are two avenues we can choose to follow. We can nurse a sense of total despair, leaving ourselves open to what might be years of suffering from troubled emotions. Or we can shift our focus from the physical realm and place it on the spiritual. Even after many disillusioning experiences, the apostle Paul chose the latter path. He knew that if he chose to derive his comfort from this world, it either would not come or it would be temporal at best.

Jesus Christ, the incarnate God, became the ultimate victim by receiving the full burden of our sin in order that its power might be put to death. When He rose from the grave He proved triumphant. Then, inviting us to let Him live in our hearts, He promised that we too could find rest from sin's curse. As Christians we cannot necessarily insulate ourselves from the world's pain, but we can lay claim to His promise that our struggles are temporary. One day we will reign with Him in glory.

SHOULD OVERCOMERS EVER CONFRONT?

The major thrust of this chapter has been to examine the attitudes one can adopt as he seeks to develop the overcomer's mind-set. Whereas circumstances cannot be altered, it is possible to learn to live in victory by yielding to Christ's empowerment. But what should be done with the person who has inflicted harm? Is it best to walk away from such people, or should they be confronted?

In certain instances confrontation is impossible. For example, the harsh treatment some of my clients have received occurred thirty of more years before they came to me for counsel. The individuals who harmed them either were dead or their whereabouts were unknown. In those cases resolution had to be primarily an internal matter.

Also, there are instances in which the harming person is so far removed from the individual's life—or is so unapproachable—that efforts to confront him are unwarranted. In some cases trying to confront the person openly would require so much obsessional effort that it would do more harm than good. Or a confrontation might create greater frustration, particularly if the person one wants to confront is likely to react with denial or belligerence.

But confrontation would be indicated in two major instances. If a genuine possibility exists that a broken relationship can be restored, confrontation should be made. Confrontation is indicated also when difficult emotions, such as resentment or depression, refuse to go away. Although it is always a good idea to adjust one's inner thoughts and attitudes, confrontation can bring an external adjustment that makes life easier to bear.

Keep in mind that the purpose of confrontation is not revenge. Hebrews 10:30 makes clear that each wrongdoer will eventually have to answer to God for misdeeds: "For we know Him who said, 'Vengeance is Mine, I will repay.'" Knowing that God will justly deal with sin, we should remember that the purpose of confrontation is healing. We need also to remember that there is no ironclad guarantee that the one being confronted will repent. Satisfaction can be found simply in knowing that one's feelings and needs have been heard.

Confrontation can be varied. An adult son or daughter can explain to a parent how trauma from the past caused him pain and ask that new adult-to-adult communication be established. A victim of a crime might face the criminal and explain the adjustments he had to make as a result of the crime. A family member might confront a substance-abusing relative to emphasize how many have suffered as a result of his behavior and to insist that the abuser receive treatment for the addiction. A brow-beaten wife might tell her husband that though she is willing to cooperate fully in fulfilling her wifely role, she will not sit idly by when abusive behavior occurs.

By expressing hurts and needs, individuals can extinguish uncomfortable emotions. As they express a belief in their innate worth and convictions, satisfaction can come. The experience can be a legitimate step in developing the overcomer's mind-set and growing into a position of peace with the past.

NINE

YIELDING TO GOD'S SOVEREIGNTY

With startling swiftness he had sunk to depths lower than he or any of his friends might have imagined. Once a prominent spiritual leader and a powerful business tycoon, Job was now banished from his community to live in the junkyard outside the city gates. The sores covering his body were so grotesque that he was unrecognizable to longstanding friends. His physical pain knew no respite, and he felt disgust at his pitiable appearance. But worse, he was reeling in shock and grief over the deaths of his seven sons and three daughters. Few things will bring a man down more quickly than the loss of a child, and Job was grieving the loss of all of his children. His mental torment and physical distress continued for days and weeks, perhaps much longer. Making matters worse, though Job's friends at first seemed anxious to help him, eventually they gave him additional pain when they accused him of hidden sins against God. Depressed and disillusioned, Job could only hope that God would watch over him. He wanted to trust God even though he did not understand why God permitted such sorrow to come into his life.

Job communicated his distress in heavenward cries. In effect he was asking God, "How long will I suffer? What did I do to deserve this misery? Didn't you make a mistake?" Then in Job 38-39 God's response is recorded. It was the *last* response Job might have anticipated:

Where were you when I laid the foundation of the earth? Tell Me, if you have understanding, who set its measurements, since you know? Or who stretched the line on it? On what were its bases sunk? Or who laid its cornerstone, when the morning stars sang together, and all the sons of God shouted for joy? . . . Have you entered into the springs of the sea? Or have you walked in the recesses of the deep? Have the gates of death been revealed to you? Or have you seen the gates of deep darkness? Have you understood the expanse of the earth? Tell Me, if you know all this. (38:4-7, 16-18)

God's words were not words of consolation!

What was God's message to Job? Surely He was not insensitive to Job's misery—His grace assures us of that. God spoke as He did to teach Job that if he was to learn to handle bitter feelings, he must first respect God's sovereign right to rule in any way He deems appropriate (fig. 9.1).

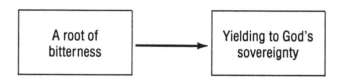

Figure 9.1

God is sovereign. He owes us nothing: not a reason, not an explanation, not a favor. He is creator and owner of all things, and we are the ones who owe Him. When problems arise, it is not our place to make God fit our mold; rather, it is His prerogative to shape the molds any way He chooses. Knowing this knocks our egos down a few notches, but if we can incorporate into our thinking an appreciation of His sovereignty, ultimately it will encourage us as we seek emotional healing.

Psychological insights alone do not represent the ultimate solution for personal struggles. Though such insights are helpful, man's wisdom is never final. Instead, psychological healing comes full circle when one submits to the power of God. We are spiritual beings first, and our efforts to make sense of problems are incomplete if we do not incorporate spiritual truth. Consequently, a powerful understanding of His nature must be in place to undergird psychological insights. But therein lies a problem. Many individuals, particularly those who have suffered psychologically, have difficulty coming to terms with God. Typically they make the mistake of trying to comprehend God through an interpretation of earth's events rather than by interpreting earth's events through a comprehension of God. They put the cart before the horse. The result is usually bitterness.

When we have made strides in incorporating Scripture's answers to our unmet needs, our ability to yield to God's sovereignty will increase.

Knowing of *God's acceptance* of us, we will feel confident that His desire always is to draw us close to Him. God is never inconsistent within Himself, so that even though we may fear the awesomeness of His character, we can be assured that He cares for us as no one else.

Living in *the privilege of choices* will cause us to understand the breadth of free will. Knowing the premium that God places on freedom, we can appreciate how He Himself is to be regarded as One not bounded by constraints. And since He is the ultimate power, subject to no one's restrictions, He has the final choice in all matters. We would be attempting to control Him if by our lack of understanding we sought to restrict His free movement.

By living with God's *gift of strength* we can find comfort in His willingness to share what He is with us. Rather than using His might against us, He is pleased to give us the ability to rise above sin's stains, just as He is above them.

Richness in experiences will cause us to have a balanced understanding of emotions. Though we still feel confused and fearful when we do not understand God, if we have richness of emotional experience, negative feelings will not be dominant. We will know joy and hope as well, and consequently will be glad that we are ruled by such a powerful sovereign.

An *eternal perspective* will remind us that God will not always be in the position of directing His character against sin. Just as there was once a time when sin did not exist, a time is coming when sin will be totally absent. At that point we will be in perfect harmony with God, and He will have no reason to show the mighty wrath that presently confuses us. The resolution of unmet needs can lead to yielding to God's sovereignty (fig. 9.2).

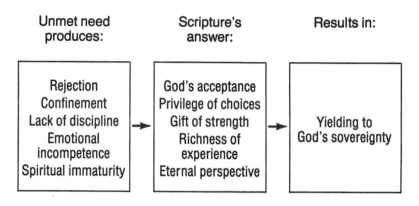

Unmet need produces:	Scripture's answer:	Results in:
Rejection Confinement Lack of discipline Emotional incompetence Spiritual immaturity	God's acceptance Privilege of choices Gift of strength Richness of experience Eternal perspective	Yielding to God's sovereignty

Figure 9.2

KEY TRAITS OF GOD

As we grow to respect God's sovereignty and know His nature, our ability to cope with psychological pain will be heightened. J. I. Packer boldly states in *Knowing God* that "when a man knows God, losses and 'crosses' cease to matter to him; what he has gained simply banishes these things from his mind."[1]

By becoming acquainted with God intimately, we will come to be directed by a conception of His greatness. Pain may remain, but it will be experienced in the perspective of God's enormity—and thus will be manageable. Because we will have made ourselves aware of the characteristics of God, we will have come to a better understanding of His perfect right to sovereignty.

1. J. I. Packer, *Knowing God* (Downers Grove, Ill.: InterVarsity, 1973), p. 23.

GOD IS ETERNAL

God's eternity is difficult to explain because our rational minds insist on believing only what can be measured. But the very definition of eternity defies human reasoning, because it transcends anything measurable. When we say that God is eternal, we mean that He always has been, always will be, and is now as He ever was. The qualities He possessed before the universe came into existence are the same qualities He has possessed throughout mankind's history and will possess during our future existence with Him in heaven. He is unaffected by time and the events occurring within time.

When God spoke with Moses at the burning bush, He called Himself Yahweh, or Jehovah, meaning "I am." He wanted Moses to understand that He is self-existent, arising from nothing, without beginning or end. The name communicated His total self-sufficiency, indicating that He has no need for human counsel. He is "I am," accountable to no one, for no one even approaches His status. He wanted Moses—and through Moses all mankind—to understand that He cannot be explained by nature's laws or man's reasoning. He transcends all that we are and all that surrounds us.

No wonder we can be confused by God's ways. Our perspective of time is exceedingly limited, and our understanding of how events fit into God's eternal scheme is shadowy. Our finiteness keeps us from being able to reconcile human events in the way that God does. What appears strange or cruel to us seems that way because we cannot place it in the context of eternity. If a man treated his family derogatorily, causing anguish for years to come, his son might interpret that behavior as a sign that God had lost touch with the family's concerns. The son might be tempted to believe that God was not aware of his family's distress or that He did not care about it. But in fact God was aware of every detail in that family's life. He had a full picture of how those events came to be and could even trace the roots of the father's behavior through the generations to Adam and Eve's original sin. It is the ultimate absurdity for us to presume that God does wrong when He allows pain. God has an eternal perspective, and He sees exactly where each behavior is leading. He knows exactly what the conclusion will be.

Knowing that God is eternal, we can be assured that His superiority is so vast that He is not threatened in the least by events that seem to us to be cruel or painful. Just as surely as He has planned the beginning of time and the end of time, He is in command of every event in between. Therefore, we can be confident that even "unexplainable" things are a part of an unfolding process controlled by Him.

GOD IS JUST

Talk with any criminal attorney, eavesdrop on any group of convicted felons, listen to the musings of appeals court judges, and you will learn that our system of law is wildly inconsistent. The punishment a person receives for a crime can be determined by any number of factors: the mood of the judge, the ability of a lawyer to present evidence, the region of the nation in which the crime was committed, the mixture of personalities on the jury, and the biases of the legislators who created the law. That explains why two people convicted of the same crime can be sentenced to widely differing punishments. The human system of justice is never close to true justice because so many subjective features exist. But the same cannot be said of God's system of justice.

All of Scripture points to the truth that God is an administrator of true justice. When we say that God is just, we mean that He is full of perfect wisdom. He is the author and possessor of all truth. His character is good through and through. He loves righteousness. He knows that evil exists; in fact, He temporarily allows it. But He has implemented a plan to deal appropriately with evil. Although injustice is allowed its time, He maintains the right to execute discipline and punishment in whatever fashion He chooses. And His decisions are always correct.

Through mankind's free choice to respond to sin, wickedness entered the world. And although the vile nature of sin clearly indicates that the sinner deserves to be destroyed totally and then cast eternally from the presence of God, God's desire to love allows sin to continue for a time until mankind is given the chance to choose to receive love for eternity. In the meantime, because God will not allow sin to run rampant without consequences, He has put in place consequences (mild in comparison to what we deserve) that apply to Adam and all his descendants. Throughout the Old Testament we are told of instances of the perpetuation of sin followed by the administration of consequences. And when mankind sufficiently proved itself incapable of responding to God's just ways, God finally intervened in sin's path and provided the perfect payment for evil in the person of Jesus Christ. Once Jesus accepted the full punishment of sin on our behalf at the cross, God then declared that anyone giving total allegiance to Him would be pronounced justly redeemed. That is why salvation is called justification. Christ makes us just so that we can commune eternally with a just God.

The truth of God's just nature leads to two conclusions. First, whatever historical events He allows are carefully considered as a part of His calculated scheme. Second, payment for injustice will be delivered, and it will always be correct. Though we are not wrong to bemoan our suffering—after all, it *does* hurt!—we must acknowledge that any pain is part of the just consequences of mankind's fall into sin. And we can also be certain that God's mercy has kept our pain from being as awful as it could be. When we suffer we are experiencing a small taste of God's justice so that we might be driven toward God, appealing to the salvation found in Jesus Christ. If God neglected to show a measure of His justice against sin, we would never be motivated to seek Him. He would be acting like a parent who allows his child to spend his childhood with no word of reproach. The outcome for that child will be far more painful and disastrous than it would have been if the child had been allowed to experience the temporary suffering produced by parental discipline. The same is true of mankind in general.

GOD IS INFALLIBLE

Closely related to the justice of God is His infallibility. To be infallible is to be perfect in every respect. It means not only that God never makes errors, but that His perfection is so complete that He is incapable of making errors. His design of creation is flawless, and even with the introduction of sin, all events should be construed as being an integral part of His master plan.

Individuals who harbor resentments against God or who assume that He is incapable of handling problems think of God as being very small. Whatever is included in such an image is so grossly wrong it is bound to result in an extreme sense of futility. To believe that God is fallible is to discredit any truth that might be gleaned from the Bible, for one could not trust that the Bible was complete. Nor could one believe in the reality of the incarnation of God in the Person of Jesus Christ, for a weak deity would not have been able to intervene in the course of humanity in that way. Similarly, all of Christ's healings and miracles would be subject to doubt, as would the authority of His teaching. Christ's substitutionary death would be seen as not necessarily enough to redeem us from sin. There would be no guarantee that at the end of time God would unequivocally conquer and judge sin, which in turn would mean that the believer's hope of a future in heaven would be dashed. In short, if one chooses to disbelieve the infallibility of God, one forfeits all hope that suffering will one day cease. The daily struggles one faces in this life would merely be sadistic torture by a God who has let matters slip from his hands.

Logic says that if we are to explain creation and the existence of life, we must concede that God possesses a mind more powerful than thousands upon thousands of complex computers. But unlike computers, which can malfunction, God's intelligence never experiences "downtime." An error-prone mind could not have conceived the notion of suspending stars and planets and moons literally in the middle of thin air (which He also spoke into being). It could not have placed our planet at the precisely correct distance from the sun, or have caused it to rotate at exactly the correct speed. Perfect calculation was required to formulate the complex combination of atmospheric gases and elements necessary to sustain life for the hundreds of thousands of life forms on the planet.

These phenomena, and millions more, *must* have come forth from a Mind so wise that it is beyond reproach.

But humanistic philosophy, which is compelled to elevate man's reasoning above God's, attempts to "expose" God's weakness by pointing to imperfections in nature and in human behavior, saying, "If God is so perfect, why do we have any of this?" Such cynicism is motivated by man's craving to rationalize his wisdom as being greater than God's. (This tendency has its origin in Genesis 3:5.) An alternative explanation for so-called imperfections in the creation can be given that does not discredit the notion of God's infallibility: Our freedom to choose sin—and thus its curse—is part of God's perfect design, and though we have made a mess of things, it is unquestionable that one day He will restore His creation to His high standards. Given the option of following sinners who arrogantly seek to play God, or of believing in a God who chooses to allow us to live for a time within the consequences of free will, I choose the latter. Nothing else makes sense.

GOD IS BENEVOLENT

To understand God's right to sovereignty, we must familiarize ourselves with the profound truth that love is the essence of God's being. The apostle Paul explained that God draws us to Him in salvation "because of His great love with which He loved us" (Ephesians 2:4). It was God's overwhelming love that caused Him to create us in His image that we might have fellowship with Him. And that same love causes Him to suspend full judgment upon sin until sufficient time has passed to allow individuals to choose freely to respond to Him with their lives. God's abiding love for us is the ultimate quality that establishes Him as the only One who can be counted on to rule our lives with absolute authority.

Consider this analogy. In my opinion there are only two humans suited to "rule" my daughter: my wife and myself. No one else has the love for her that we do. Our parental love qualifies us to hold a position of authority in her life appropriate for no one else. On a higher plane, no one other than

God is suited to make decisions regarding the human race. He alone possesses the love required to be an appropriate Authority.

The implication of this notion is powerful: God loves the human race so deeply that only He can be trusted to decide how life should unfold. His love compels Him to consider every circumstance we face. He has no desire that we should suffer, save that it be suffering that can lead us to Him. He never wishes harm on anyone—particularly harm of the frivolous variety. I have spoken with many bitter individuals, who if they were truthful would admit that they wished harm upon those who had wronged them. Likewise, I have spoken with many guilt-laden individuals who, because of past sins, wish condemnation upon themselves. If I suggest that they leave the judgment of others or even of themselves to God because He will seek what is right, they hesitate: "It sounds too simplistic to say that." But indeed, that is exactly what should be done. Particularly when we see a wrong, we humans are quite limited in our ability to love. A few of us may be able to philosophize about the God-given worth of each person, but when we are really pressed to make decisions about wrongdoers, we are not disposed to filter our decisions through love.

But God is not like humans. Love so permeates God's character that it draws Him toward the vilest of evildoers. Romans 5:8 communicates God's incredible love: "But God demonstrates His own love toward us, in that while we were yet sinners, Christ died for us." God's ability to reign will never be adversely influenced by the wrongs we commit. If He has any bias, it is toward mercy rather than harshness.

The love of God means that He has an affinity for us that is consistent in spite of our inconsistencies. We do not always perceive this affinity, because we are so intent on fitting God and the events of our lives into our own molds. But it is not so with God. Romans 8:38-39 assures us that there is nothing on earth or nothing in the heavens that can cause God's love to cease. To prove the point, God delegated Jesus Christ to live among us to become the embodiment of that love, so that through Him we could know its fullness.

Our Response to God's Sovereignty

As the awareness we have of God's right to be sovereign grows, that sovereignty will demand a response of us. We can choose either to ignore or negate the might of God—and thus look to human resources for direction in life—or we can bow to God in submission, committing ourselves to a lifelong yielding to His rule. Since the first choice leads to uncertainty and a lack of absolutes, it is wise to yield gladly to God by setting self-will aside.

The decision to let God be God has several implications for those trying to put psychological traumas to rest.

IMPLICATION 1: EMOTIONAL HEALING WILL BE GUIDED BY HUMILITY

No person can contemplate the qualities of God without soon facing his own frailty. Romans 1:18-20 explains that within each person is an awareness of God's righteousness and man's unrighteousness. No one can claim exemption from this insight, for it is indelibly imprinted in the conscience, leaving each of us "without excuse" (v. 20). But there is a quality inside each person that can cause resistance to this revelation. That quality is pride. Since the day Satan enticed Eve and then Adam to try to "be like God" (Genesis 3:5), every person has had an intense struggle with sinful pride. No one lives without this problem. Although we often think of pride as being exhibited by conceit and bravado, it is much broader. Sinful pride is defined as preoccupation with self's importance, needs, and desires. It is manifested in each person every day in a variety of ways.

Beginning in early childhood, each person is hungry for self-direction. Young children receive no instruction to be aggressive, to pout, or to be easily frustrated. They naturally act this way because they are born into sin. As they grow older they may learn more refinement in social skills, but the root of selfishness never leaves. This self-preoccupation is at the center of the adult behavior that leads to tension: worry, criticism, insecurity, impatience, insensitivity, pouting, defensiveness, bitterness, envy, laziness. In fact, any deficiency in communication, behavior, or emotions ultimately can be traced to the presence of sinful pride. Pride is more prevalent and cancerous than any other problem known to mankind.

It is no coincidence that Scripture repeatedly instructs individuals to set self-preoccupations aside in favor of the direction of God. Proverbs 3:5-6 tells us, "Trust in the Lord with all your heart, and do not lean on your own understanding. In all your ways acknowledge Him, and He will make your paths straight." The passage communicates the fact that when we are left to resolve struggles on our own, inevitably we will make a mess of matters, for our understanding is stained. Only God is wise enough to direct us, and we must be willing to admit it. James 4:6 is even more direct: "God is opposed to the proud, but gives grace to the humble." By indulging self-serving thoughts, we place ourselves in opposition to God and thus doom ourselves to live strictly within our own finite reasoning.

Therefore, rather than giving prominence to self-preoccupation, we should seek peace through humility. Humility implies a lack of excessive concern for self, exemplified by a willingness to let go of the craving to be in control. It does not imply a total lack of self-regard, for even Jesus took self-protective measures at times. It does recognize self's frailness and is willing to accept one's strength as limited. Moreover, it freely acknowledges God's power as far superior than one's own.

Humility is not always easy for the person seeking to overcome problems from the past. This is because our troubles inevitably cause us to focus on self's needs and hurts, which when not readily eased can lead to self-preoccupation. Yet when we acknowledge that such a preoccupation leads only to prolonged emotional duress, we will find that humility is indeed a healthier avenue. We will have the peace of leaving the ultimate problem-solving tasks to almighty God.

IMPLICATION 2: ACCEPT THE INEVITABILITY OF SUFFERING

I am aware that it is unpopular to suggest that we allow for suffering. Modern positive thinking enthusiasts try to entice us into believing that if only we would choose to be "on top of it all," we could leave our worries behind. If we choose to be strong, we will be strong. The implication is that we can rid ourselves of negative experiences if we merely apply ourselves. Though I believe that individuals can find increasing happiness and strength, I assume that those qualities are by-products of submission to God rather than the result of positive thinking. And I believe also that happiness and strength can be available to us even in the midst of suffering. If we naively adhered to the "think positive, be prosperous" philosophy, we would be forced to conclude that suffering is entirely the result of thinking small. We would then be sidestepping the reality of God's hatred of sin.

Like it or not, we will each suffer, some more severely than others. Humility leads us to recognize that as long as we are sinners living in a sin-cursed world, problems will be a predictable part of life. No family will be free of at least some dissension. No childhood will ever unfold as neatly as child development manuals prescribe. No Christian group will perfectly meet its members' needs. No individual will escape experiencing improper emotions. We will all suffer, either by someone else's hand or by our own. Because God's justice demands consequences for wrongdoing, some form of pain will be felt by each of us. The more we are able to accept this unflattering truth willingly, the less shocked we will be by problems, and the more objective we will be in seeking God's resolution of our problems.

At first glance, it seems strange to argue that accepting suffering can help us make peace with the past. Some even assume that accepting suffering will create a martyr complex in us. But that is not necessarily what will happen. Do you recall how you feel the morning after a day of vigorous exercise? If you are like me, your bones crack as you crawl out of bed. Your back screams with pain when you bend over to put on your shoes. You cringe at the prospect of physical labor. Your body is suffering the consequence of being overextended, and pain is the predictable result. Although some things can be done to ease the pain, you are still faced with choices regarding your mental outlook. You can choose to be angry, whining, and complaining about your aches—and thus accentuate your discomfort. Or you can choose to accept the fact that you will feel sore, while at the same time being determined to carry on with the normal activities of the day. You neither ignore the pain nor relish it but rather accept it as real.

In the same way, when we accept the fact that general sin produces discomfort, we learn to press forward with goal-directed behavior in spite of setbacks that occur. We should not expect to relish the pain, for that would be denying human emotions. Yet we need not delude ourselves that pain can somehow be sidestepped. In His prayer in the garden before His arrest and crucifixion, Jesus Christ felt the overbearing psychological trauma arising from the prospect of suffering under the load of the world's sin. Christ made no attempt to deny the presence of deep agony, yet He concluded "not My will, but Thine be done" (Luke 22:42). Christ hated the suffering imposed on Him, but He resolved His grief by submitting to the sovereignty of the Father. Acquiescing to that sovereignty, Christ concluded that His suffering would not be in vain. As we follow His lead, we too can conclude that though we suffer, our suffering is not purposeless.

IMPLICATION 3: FAITH BECOMES A CORE INGREDIENT IN PERSONAL CONTENTMENT

As you read these pages, you are probably sitting in a chair. Though you may have thought little about the act of settling yourself into that chair, you were actually exercising faith. You looked at the chair, thought of your desire to get off your feet, and then put your whole weight onto the chair, assuming that it would be strong enough to support you. You had acted in like manner so many thousands of times before that your faith in the chair's ability to hold you up had become automatic. Unless you had recently fallen out of a chair, you acted without question.

I wish our faith in God could be so simple and automatic. But is it not. We usually insist that the things we trust be undeniably proved first. And because God often makes no attempt to prove Himself before asking for faith, we balk. We forget that we are the ones in need of Him, not the other way around. When we stubbornly resist God and attempt to force Him to come down to our level, we create trouble for ourselves. We are like a person with aching feet who will not sit in an armchair until someone produces blueprints proving that the chair has a sturdy design. Rest might be readily available, but it cannot be experienced until faith is exercised.

Unlike the physical, material things we trust each day, God is spiritual. He cannot be seen or touched in the way we see and touch the objects that surround us. Therefore, we are required to exercise the spiritual side of ourselves before we can find peace in Him. But when our spirits have been bruised or even broken, relating in faith to the ultimate spiritual Person is unnatural.

Yet faith *can* be experienced as we learn to embrace the grandeur of His character. Recognizing His superiority highlights our own weakness and will in turn prompt us to recognize that it is unwise to choose faith in human ability over faith in God's abilities. Our failures and misjudgments are so common that they prove how incapable we are of self-government. The apostle Paul confessed, "He has said to me, 'My grace is sufficient for you, for power is perfected in weakness' " (2 Corinthians 12:9). Comparing our frailty to His enormity creates dependency on Him, resulting in submissive contentment.

IMPLICATION 4: OUR GRATITUDE FOR SALVATION CAN MULTIPLY

I have a friend, Bill, who broke his neck on the ski slopes of Colorado. He tells of the terror he felt when he realized that he had no feeling or body movement from his neck to his toes. It is impossible for me to give an adequate description of his emotional state as he waited helplessly for the medical team. Can you imagine what you might think about if you were in that position? Bill wondered if he would die or, worse, if he would be totally paralyzed. He imagined the pressures that would be placed on his wife, Deeann, and he agonized about the trauma his three daughters would feel. Thoughts of God flowed—and admittedly not all were "spiritual." Here he was, a well-adjusted Christian man—successful in the business world, content with his family, faithful in service to his church—lying in total numbness in the snow, feeling small and helpless.

After traction, surgery, and months of physical rehabilitation, Bill regained most of his strength and senses. He is back on the job, can play games with his daughters, and has resumed his activities in the church. But he is not the same person. Oh, he looks the same and talks the same, and he has not changed any major beliefs or undergone an overhaul of his personality. But he feels his emotions more passionately, and he has a higher appreciation for his health, his family, and his friends. When he contemplates spiritual ideas, they run more deeply. He lives on an altogether richer plane.

If you asked Bill what he appreciates most about the events surrounding his recovery, he would certainly applaud the people who rallied around him, prayed for him, and encouraged him. He would have no trouble giving credit to his wife, his doctors, and his nurses for their efforts in pulling him through. But Bill admits he has a special place in his heart for the men who provided the first step toward recovery, the paramedics. He deeply appreciates how quickly they arrived on the scene, how accurately they diagnosed his damage, and how expertly they tended to his needs. Anything less than perfection from them would have cost him his life. Had they not been so skilled, none of the other people could have given all they did. He daily feels thanks for them, yet he knows that a simple "thank you" does not capture the fullness of his heart.

When people have had difficulties in the past, they can feel totally paralyzed and helpless to recover from their burdens, just as Bill did as he lay on the side of the mountain. They are painfully aware of their inability to right the wrongs and are susceptible to despair. But when they acknowledge that the God of all creation in the full authority of His sovereign might sent Jesus Christ to perform the precise act necessary to deliver them from their pain, they feel a thanks that defies expression. This gladness of heart swells even more when they realize that the Holy Spirit was sent to perform daily surgery on emotional wounds. Like the man lying broken in the snow, the individual broken by wrongful experiences can learn to live with a richness of life after he receives this healing from the God who cares.

Humility can lead us to the conclusion that God is so great and we are so wretched that He should feel no obligation to descend to our pitiable lives—that we do not really deserve God. Yet the entire message of the Bible can be summarized in the idea that though God in His sovereignty abhors sin, His grace compels Him to seek and to save those who are willing to turn their lives over to Him. We know that God had nothing to gain by sending Jesus Christ to take our sins to the cross. But such knowledge can cause us to shake our heads in awe and wonder as we study the gift so undeservedly given at Calvary. Like my friend Bill, the awareness of our total need for His saving hand can cause us to feel enough gratitude to last an eternity. Knowing the immensity of God's character makes us feel privileged that He Himself would carry us into recovery.

cease being grace. The person living in grace learns to live under a completely different rule, one which is directed by an inner feeling of purpose rather than by an external sense of duty. One's power for living is totally God-given and Spirit-directed. The self's sense of worth is deep, but it has nothing to do with meeting standards. A feeling of personal cleanness is dominant in spite of continued brushes with sin. Hope dominates the personality as the reality of victory over sin sinks in.

When we continue in the guilt and tension caused by unmet needs, we have difficulty understanding grace, much less living in it. But when we learn to apply Scripture's answers to those unmet needs, grace becomes more natural to our way of life.

By believing in *God's acceptance* as the answer to human rejection, we take a vital first step toward grace. Though human interactions may have created in us a feeling of unworthiness, we can be assured that such a feeling is counter to God's message. When we choose to believe His acceptance is real, our minds become prepared to accept the full message of grace.

The *privilege of choices* is actually a provision of grace. If God so desired, He could choose to place us under a yoke of obligation, forcing us to conform to His dictates before He allowed us salvation. But to do so would imply conditional love. Therefore, He has taken the risk of removing the demands of duty, extending choices to us instead. When we learn to live with the privilege of choices, we can comprehend grace experientially.

God offers the *gift of strength* as an antidote for our lack of inner control. Knowing that our bent toward sin disrupts our ability to carry out the life-style He prefers, He gives the Holy Spirit to help carry us through our difficulties. The more we open our minds and emotions to His enablement, the more we will be filled with firsthand, experiential knowledge of grace.

The richness of experience that is derived from gaining familiarity with our emotions draws us subjectively into the beauty of God's design for us. We become able not only to

TEN
LIVING IN GRACE

In chapter 4 we discussed how unmet needs can leave individuals vulnerable to debilitating guilt. Although a healthy repentant type of guilt exists that should not be brushed aside, persons with past problems often lack the necessary balance to manage this emotion. False guilt thus gains a foothold in the personality, creating undue strain on a life already under pressure.

But when Scripture's answers are applied to unmet needs, false guilt can be mastered, freeing individuals to live in composure rather than under tension. The quality that can be learned as the counter to false guilt is grace (fig. 10.1). When grace is experienced, lasting peace can be found.

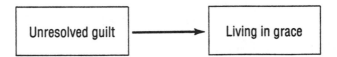

Figure 10.1

Lewis Sperry Chafer defined grace as "pure unrecompensed kindness and favor."[1] Grace cannot possibly be earned because any requirement of performance would cause it to

1. Lewis Sperry Chafer, *Grace* (Findlay, Ohio: Dunham Publishing, 1922), p. xv.

know about the goodness of the Christian life but to feel it as well. That in turn increases our ability to live in grace, for grace will have become not only something to intellectualize about but something to be experienced richly .

As we gain *eternal perspective* we learn that there is much, much more to God than just His contention with sin. As we begin to soak in the enormity of His creativeness and the expanse of His dwelling place, we are awed by His willingness to extend salvation to us. Such wonder increases our capacity for grace.

Incorporating Scripture's answers to our unmet needs can result in freedom from guilt (fig. 10.2).

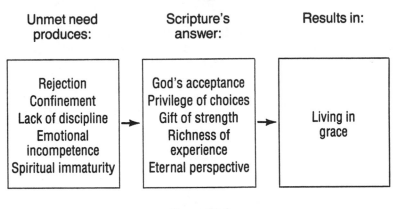

Unmet need produces:	Scripture's answer:	Results in:
Rejection Confinement Lack of discipline Emotional incompetence Spiritual immaturity	God's acceptance Privilege of choices Gift of strength Richness of experience Eternal perspective	Living in grace

Figure 10.2

What Grace Is

The resolution of unmet needs prepares our minds to respond to the grace of God. But to do so successfully, we must know what grace is. As we analyze its qualities, we discover that grace is a multidimensional trait.

GRACE IS UNMERITED LOVE

A certain type of love appears when the object of love is consistently lovable. For example, each of us has known that extra feeling of attraction when a child has behaved exceptionally well or when a spouse has done an especially nice favor. It is easy to love under those circumstances. In fact, only the most hardened person would fail to love those who treated him with unusual kindness.

But another type of love exists when the recipient is not only imperfect, but ugly and disrespectful. Whereas this love —unmerited love—is unnatural to man, it is an integral part of God's grace. God's unmerited love is so supernatural and so different from man's that it transcends the parameters of human emotion. We humans have no ability to initiate such a love, nor do we possess the right to demand it. Yet God is not bound by frailty, and He is so consumed with the desire to share Himself with us that He offers His love freely.

God's grace has nothing to do with our deservedness but everything to do with His greatness. It is His "no strings attached" gift of pure and undefiled benevolence. It is *always* a gift since it cannot be bought or earned. And what is more, it will never be retracted, for God's grace eliminates the need for records of right or wrong. Furthermore, it is not motivated by reason, for reason's logic (at least as man knows it) refutes the legitimacy of grace. Rather, grace is so forgiving that it completely overlooks the inhibiting boundaries of rationalism. The ultimate expression of this unmerited love came in the incarnation of the agent of grace, Jesus Christ. John 1:9-12 declares that Christ came into the world to shed light upon its darkness. His singular mission was to redeem the lost world unto God. Yet the world did not receive Him. He was mocked, His teaching and authority were challenged, His love and forgiveness were questioned, and He was killed. But amazingly, even when He was being nailed to the cross, a cross He did not deserve, He maintained His grace, praying, "Father, forgive them; for they do not know what they are doing" (Luke 23:34). In the midst of mankind's most unspeakable crime against God, Jesus Christ was consumed with an unrelenting love for lost mankind. Then when He rose from the grave, conquering death, He invited all who would receive Him as Savior to enter into an eternity of God's love. No conditions were laid out; the only requirement was to receive it.

For individuals who have agonized over painful problems from the past, God's grace seems too good to be true. The notion of a love that records no demerits stands in direct contrast to the experiences they have had, which emphasized conditions. They have memories of human encounters in which no love or only an "earned" love was given and find God's love difficult to conceptualize. If these people are to receive grace, they must change the mind-set to realize that love can indeed be given without preconditions. They will be helped to make this adjustment if a human agent of grace steps forward to illustrate God's ways.

I am deeply moved by the story of a college student, Wade, who taught grace to an impoverished inner-city grade-school boy, Alberto. Wade's part-time job was to drive a school bus each morning and afternoon throughout the toughest part of the city. Alberto was the one child—there is always one in the crowd—who distinguished himself by outlandish behavior. He pulled the girls' hair, hid their books, shouted defiantly when he was told to be quiet. But in spite of Alberto's rebelliousness, Wade felt a deep love for him. Since Alberto was the last child off the bus each day, Wade looked forward to the chance for uninterrupted talk with his feisty little buddy.

One cold November afternoon, Wade noticed that Alberto was not wearing a winter jacket. When he inquired about it, he learned that Alberto did not even *own* a jacket. After he completed his bus run, Wade picked up Alberto at his run-down shack of a home and took the boy to the store to buy a coat that would last through two winters. Then he took him to his own modest apartment and fed him supper. This encounter sparked a long-term relationship, resulting in many hours spent one-on-one. What is more, Wade became acquainted with Alberto's pitiable family life. Several times he ministered to the boy's alcoholic mother, helping her cope with problems involving relatives and neighbors, who were prone to fighting. He witnessed the harsh way Alberto's family communicated with one another and saw firsthand how poverty can cause human beings to turn against each other while they scrounge for food and money. As often as possible, Wade sought to befriend Alberto and his family.

In time, Wade began witnessing to Alberto about Jesus Christ. He knew that his friend needed to know that the God who gave him life loved him dearly. When Wade explained how Jesus Christ died for him so that he could live in eternity with God, Alberto asked a simple question, "Does Jesus love me the same way you love me?" When Wade responded that Jesus loved him far more, Alberto smiled and said, "If He loves me more than you do, how could I not love Him back?" Though he was poor by the world's standards, Alberto's experience with his bus driver had made him wealthy in the knowledge of God's grace.

Not all people have the good fortune of having friends who enable them to experience the grace of God so richly. In fact, many individuals must shed memories of bitter experiences at the hands of the authority figures most significant to them. Yet they can find solace in the truth that God's grace remains, however appropriately or inappropriately human beings act. John 3:16 eloquently summarizes the grace of God: "For God so loved the world, that He gave His only begotten Son, that whosoever believes in Him should not perish, but have eternal life."

GRACE IS GOD'S SUSTAINING POWER

Envision a child whose entire family has died. Then picture the love and compassion an adoptive father and mother have for that child as they bring him into their home to live permanently as one of their children. This is saving grace. Then imagine the child's struggle with his sense of loss, troublesome emotions, and peer relations. When his new parents consistently assist him in those times of struggle with love and nurturing, they are exhibiting sustaining grace.

God's sustaining grace is His continuing willingness to provide the necessary strength and guidance in an individual's daily circumstances. God recognizes that no human has the natural capacity to live a life pleasing to Him, so in love He Himself fills the Christian with the ability to live in His will. This concept is captured in Galatians 2:20: "I have been crucified with Christ; and it is no longer I who live, but Christ lives in me; and the life which I now live in the flesh I live by faith in the Son of God, who loved me, and delivered Himself up for me." God's grace enables us to overcome the tendency to err. He empowers us to be patient when we might otherwise be irritable; He empowers us to forgive in spite of our resentments; and He fills us with confidence when we might otherwise feel weak.

Because we have finite minds, it is difficult for us to comprehend the miracle that occurs when we receive God's grace. God's Holy Spirit literally takes residence inside our hearts and minds, giving new direction to our thoughts, preferences, and behavior. But because we struggle to understand the mechanics of the Holy Spirit's activity in our lives, we often ignore Him or assume that He is less than what He is—Almighty God. Thankfully, we can acknowledge that our lack of comprehension does not cause Him to retreat from our lives. Once God promises to empower us, He never retracts His word. Therefore, we can be assured that the Holy Spirit will become a real entity to us when we fully accept the promise of Christ: "I will ask the Father, and He will give you another Helper, that He may be with you forever" (John 14:16). As Christians we can have the assurance of knowing that God's Holy Spirit will provide the strength we need to overcome our troubles. Our task is to claim that strength and allow God to control our circumstances.

In order for us to make the sustaining grace of God a greater reality in our lives, we must regularly nurture a love relationship with God. His power becomes more real when He becomes more familiar to us in a personal relationship. A marriage relationship only begins with the wedding ceremony. The marriage will become strong only through consistency in communication between the new husband and wife. Similarly, our relationship with God will require daily, persistent efforts to gain familiarity with God and His ways. We need to spend time daily in prayer and Bible study. We need to worship regularly in a local church and participate in its ministries. We need to spend time in fellowship with like-minded believers. As these practices become habitual, they will strengthen the love we have toward God. As a result, we will experience an unforced capacity to derive strength from the Source of all power. God will have become a friend whose indwelling presence is natural.

GRACE IS GOD'S FUTURE PROVISION

When God offers us the gift of grace, it is for one purpose: He desires to share in a love relationship with each of us for all eternity. Grace then can be understood as a provision for our lives in the future. Grace not only saves us from our past and sustains us in the present, but it secures for us a future of bliss. In the book of Revelation, John presents a glimpse of the Christian's future home in heaven: " 'He shall wipe away every tear from their eyes; and there shall no longer be any death; there shall no longer be any mourning, or crying, or pain; the first things have passed away.' And He who sits on the throne said, 'Behold, I am making all things new' " (21:4-5).

One day each of us will stand before God to give an account for our sinful lives. In the balance will be a future existence, either with or without Him. Knowing that our past deeds are completely inadequate to convince the Judge of our right to be admitted into His presence, the Agent of grace, Jesus Christ, will step forward on our behalf and plead our case before God. Because God honors the righteousness of Jesus, He will grant eternal life to all those belonging to Him. First John 2:1-2 states, "If anyone sins, we have an Advocate with the Father, Jesus Christ the righteous; and He Himself is the propitiation for our sins." When Jesus died and rose from the grave, He guaranteed a secure future for all who committed their lives to Him as Savior, for His victory over death gave Him the right to be seated at the right hand of God, jointly reigning with Him over all creation. Because they have a perfect, worthy Advocate, Christians can know with confidence that their earthly lives of tension and distress will one day be set aside for an eternity of joy.

Every day I talk with individuals who focus on problems in the past so obsessively that they can see no hope for the future. They reason that since their histories produced misery and since they have had no success in defeating their problems, the future must also be bleak. There *is* some truth to their logic, according to purely human reasoning. Humanly speaking, there is little reason to assume that positive things will come to a life filled with negatives. But this logic does not account for the supernatural grace of God, which enables us to overcome past and present failures. Jesus Christ boldly stated, "In the world you have tribulation, but take courage; I have overcome the world" (John 16:33). Those attached to Him can be assured that they too will overcome the struggles of the world, just as He did.

Significantly, it was the apostle Paul who wrote, "Forgetting what lies behind and reaching forward to what lies ahead" (Philippians 3:13). His history was remarkable, particularly in the hatred he had demonstrated toward Christians. He had led parties of thugs who killed and maimed Jews who claimed to be followers of "The Way." If Paul had spent much time reflecting on the crimes he had committed against God's people, he would easily have sunk into the depths of shame. But fortunately he had discovered the secret of defeating the past by claiming God's provision for his future. He summarized his hope in Philippians 3:20-21: "For our citizenship is in heaven, from which also we eagerly wait for a Savior, the Lord Jesus Christ; who will transform the body of our humble state into conformity with the body of His glory."

IMPLICATION: PERFORMANCE HAS A NEW MEANING

As I drove my car one summer afternoon I was amused at the antics of a frustrated fly. Trapped in a prison of glass and steel, the fly was desperate to find his way outside. On all sides he could see the destiny he sought, but as he took flight toward it, he bumped against an unyielding shield. Stopped abruptly, he would fly toward a window in a different part of the car, only to face the same fate. No doubt the little creature was confused by the fact that he could see the outside world but was prevented by a mysterious force from actually reaching it. As long as the barrier was in place, try as hard as he could, he lacked the ability to achieve his goal.

Many people are like the fly. They have known the facts about grace for years. They have heard eloquent sermons about its wonders and repeatedly have sung hymns to God praising its virtues. They can even envision the contentment of life that would surely accompany the implementation of grace. Yet their life experiences do not reflect grace's guidance. They desire to enter a life of grace, but they are hindered by an unseen mental barrier that keeps grace from being a reality in their lives.

The barrier that obstructs individuals from experiencing grace consistently is an obsession to perform correctly. If grace represents God's unmerited love for lost humanity, the opposite of it is conditional favor based upon acceptable performance. When an individual feels that he needs to work to receive God's love, grace is no longer grace. He has reverted to living under the law, just as the Pharisees. Even though Matthew 7:1 tells us not to get caught in the trap of judging one another, we do so anyway, creating relationships that put a premium on performing "correctly."

As a six year old, I represented my first-grade class in a regional spelling bee. The boys and girls in Mrs. Spain's room had been evaluated over the course of several weeks, and to my surprise I was the best speller of the bunch. I remember the excitement I felt when Mrs. Spain and I drove to the auditorium where the spelling bee was to be held. My parents were in the audience, as were the parents of all the other participants. Being in the youngest group, I didn't have to wait long to be seated at a desk alongside the other children. We were given five words to write on a sheet of paper. Then we were asked to turn our papers into the judges, who graded them. Anyone making an error was excused, and the remaining participants were given five more words. This continued until a winner emerged. I had never had much trouble reading and writing, so I assumed that when the five-dollar prize was given, I would be the recipient. But to my dismay, the words became difficult. I made an error and was eliminated from the competition. Though I had won third prize (two one-dollar bills), as far as I was concerned I was a failure. In spite of reassurances from my mother and from Mrs. Spain, I was disgusted with myself. I had wanted to be judged the best, but I had to settle for third place.

My experience as a first grader captures the tension all humans feel over the need to perform. From earliest childhood throughout adult life, we are highly judgmental of our performance and feel distress when it is not satisfactory. All of us are prone to this tension, for each of us has an inherent insecurity that feeds the need to be somebody. No one enjoys being labeled a loser, and no one wants to be shown up by someone of greater status.

Unfortunately, in spite of our craving for superior evaluations, we are prone to performances that are not only inadequate but dismally poor. Romans 3:23 directly states that "all have sinned and fall short of the glory of God." The prophet Isaiah expressed this truth even more strongly when he wrote, "For all of us have become like one who is unclean, and all our righteous deeds are like a filthy garment" (64:6). Though each individual may have areas of special skill that bring praise and high grades, no one can claim greatness on the basis of performance, for no one has the inherent ability to achieve perfection. That is why grace is necessary.

The beauty of grace is that it will have nothing to do with the unhealthy obsession to do everything perfectly. Grace keeps no score of successes and failures. It cares nothing about one's comparative standing. It does not insist upon skilled performance. It is merely given. No records are examined, no scores are weighed. It is the consummate, unconditional gift. Just as the prodigal son found that his father was pleased to receive him fully, we too can know that God through Christ will receive us without reservation unto Himself.

When we set aside an obsession with performance, does that mean that we should pay no attention to our works? In answering a similar question, Paul wrote, "Present yourselves to God as those alive from the dead, and your members as instruments of righteousness to God" (Romans 6:13). Even though we are infinitely fortunate to receive God's grace, we are instructed to continue to allow the Holy Spirit to guide us toward righteous living. The difference comes in that we are no longer performing to prove our goodness; we are willingly allowing our lives to be conformed to His will.

When I speak at seminars and conferences, people will sometimes come up afterward and say, "When you spoke about anger, I understood myself in a different way." That encourages me without at the same time "grading" me. But invariably, there is always the person who comes up and says, "You did a good job." I am thankful for the positive feedback, but I do not take the comment seriously, because I do not speak publicly in order to receive a good "report card." If someone chooses to make a formal evaluation of my performance, they are free to do so. But I remind myself that I perform for the Lord's glory rather than for my own.

In every aspect of life we would do well to sidestep performance expectations as often as possible. We need to be concerned with living in God's will, not because of our ego needs, but out of a sheer love for God's ways. In doing so, we prepare our minds to receive the gift of grace.

ONE WHO FOUND GRACE

What if regrettable childhood experiences and later exposure to rough companions lead a man to the edge of ruin—can he discover the amazing grace of God and begin the long journey of recovery from his past? He can indeed.

John was such a man. He was born in England in 1725, the only child of a sickly mother and a merchant mariner father. His father had been reared in a religious atmosphere and was strict to the point of being harsh. But his exposure to the licentious life-style of sailors had eroded what spirituality he may once have possessed, and John knew him chiefly to be a blustery, distant parent. John's father's work required him to be away from the family's modest home for months at a time, for he sailed from Britain to the Mediterranean Sea in search of goods to bring home and sell. Each year he made two or three runs, leaving his young son at home with his mother. Frankly, the relationship between the father and mother was so strained that the father's absence was actually a relief.

The mother was of an entirely different mold, being devoutly religious and faithful to a church just up the street from their home. She sang hymns to John, taught him Bible verses, and prayed daily with him. Although John's father had always assumed that the boy would become a merchant mariner as he was, his mother had hopes of preparing him for seminary. Her influence on young John was brief, however. At the age of thirty, shortly before her son's seventh birthday, she died.

At his mother's death, John was taken in by a neighbor until his father returned from his voyage. When he received the news of his wife's death, the father showed no grief and in only a few weeks had remarried. Then he left the child with his stepmother and returned to sea. The years following were unhappy for the young boy, for John was unwanted and unloved by his stepmother. To rid herself of him, John's stepmother sent him to a boarding school for four years. The experience exposed John to rigid discipline and little kindness, leaving him feeling abandoned and rejected. While he was at school, John became fairly proficient in scholastics, but his spirit was badly bruised by frequent punishments, and he never pushed himself to reach the limits of his abilities. Rage festered within him, and he dreamed of the day he could leave the cruelty of the school. During this period the distance between John and his father grew, for their infrequent visits only reminded the boy of his father's insensitivity.

When John was eleven, his father invited him to sail with him as a cabin boy on a trading voyage through the Mediterranean. John gladly jumped at the chance to leave the hated school for a new challenge. Exposure to the coarseness of the ship's sailors did nothing to strengthen the boy at such a sensitive time in his moral development, but nonetheless John learned to enjoy the unrestrained life-style of a seaman. And in the next six years he sailed on four more such voyages. He never returned to formal education.

During his teen years, John could best be described as a boy in a tremendous moral decline. His lack of parental love and his exposure to the men of the sea gave him firsthand knowledge of the effects of sin in a person's life. Because of his mother's early spiritual influence, he had moments when he struggled with guilt over his bad habits. But because he lacked spiritual guidance, slowly he became more and more comfortable in his crudeness, and by his late teens he was hardly distinguishable from the most hardened sailor. By age sixteen he was reported to be a worthless troublemaker who frustrated anyone wanting an honest day of work from him.

At age eighteen, while he was on leave from seafaring, John was forced into the English navy by a press-gang—navy recruiters who were desperate for deckhands and capable of using any means possible to coerce a man into duty. Initially his new captain did not realize the extent of John's hostility, but he grew to resent deeply John's insubordination and vile tongue. On the voyage with the Royal Navy, John was frequently assigned the most loathsome duties and was overworked in the hope that he would learn the humility required of a crewman. When hard labor failed to gain the desired result, he was strapped in irons in the hull of the ship and given only minimal food rations for days at a time. But whenever he returned to his appointed duty, he frustrated his superiors with the same insolence and in short time was considered the sorriest man on board.

Within the year, the ship's commander found his chance to discharge John from the Navy. While the ship was in harbor for supplies, John had made a near-successful attempt to desert but was arrested and placed again in irons in the ship's hull. In the mid–1700s a man could be hanged for such an offense, so the punishment John received—a flogging—was considered merciful. Soon afterward, the captain arranged to trade John for a deckhand of a civilian merchant ship similar to the one John had sailed on in earlier years with his father. So before his twentieth birthday, John was released from military duty and set sail with his new employer for the coast of Africa in search of "cargo" to transport to North America. That simply meant John became a slave trader.

For six months the ship's crew scoured the African shores, capturing men and women and bargaining with tribal chiefs for slaves. Already possessing a hardened nature, John became even more barbarous as he learned to treat the slaves like animals. He had no compunction about beating a captive into pitiful submission, using torture if it were necessary. And when slave women boarded the ship, naked, he joined his fellow crewmen by indulging his sexual craving at their expense. Although none of the crew thought of themselves as rapists, there is no more suitable word to describe them. The crew probably had no concern about the fact that many of these women became pregnant and bore their children in hardship several months later on foreign soil. They were only concerned with momentary pleasure. But if these experiences marked the low point of John's decaying life, what followed was hardly an improvement.

As had happened previously, John's temper became so unrestrained that the ship's captain grew to hate him deeply. Sensing this, John decided to desert the ship and stay in Africa. Instead of proceeding with his mates to North America, he hired on with a slave broker, finding slaves to sell to merchants. Predictably, it was not long before he found himself in more trouble. This time he came into disfavor with his boss' common-law wife, who had him placed in chains and confined in the slaves' quarters, there to serve as a servant to slaves. He was given table scraps for food. Now he experienced the turnabout of being insulted by his African captors, absorbing beatings, and generally being treated as an animal.

Finally, after living two miserable years in Africa, he found work aboard a trading vessel stocked with gold, ivory, and slaves. This ship took him across the Atlantic to America, and once again he indulged in the sailor's life-style of drunkenness and moral filth. He seemed trapped in a personality determined to destroy him and anyone near him.

John might have continued forever in his miserable state had the captain not brought some books on board pertaining to Jesus Christ. During idle moments John read those books, and in doing so was reminded of his mother's desire for him to know God. He pictured his mother reading Bible stories and singing songs. Ashamed, he thought about his own life and compared the ways of God with his own wretchedness. Miraculously, the Holy Spirit was at work in his heart, and he was receptive.

John made the first major step toward God in his twenty-third year, as his ship was returning from America to England across the North Atlantic Sea. A tremendous storm almost sank the ship, and John's guilt caught up with him as he faced the prospect of standing before God to make an account for his life. He knew he had to make things right with God then and there, so in the midst of the raging sea he prayed to God for forgiveness and promised to live for Christ.

In the years following, John married a childhood sweetheart and made many steps forward in his morality. But knowing no other way of life, he continued three more years in the shipping business, at times still transporting slaves from Africa to North America. Though his spiritual immaturity was evidenced by the continuation of this profession, John at least refrained from drunkenness and sexual immorality. In time, as he studied the Bible and read Christian books, he became convinced of the evil of the slave industry. As a consequence, he turned his back on the sea and took a respectable land job. In years to come he became a fervent activist in the movement to abolish slavery, testifying of his experiences before Parliament.

By age thirty-three John had become deeply involved in Bible study and was considered a solid layman in his church. After much prayer and prodding by church members, he surrendered his life to preach the message of God's redemptive love. When he remembered his past experiences of wild rebellion, hate, licentiousness, and loneliness, he considered it remarkable that God would allow someone like him to be a full-time minister of the gospel. But God knew exactly what He was doing, and He gave John an unusual ability to communicate the message of salvation to people who might not listen to a typical minister. He became a great soul winner and was powerfully instrumental in the spread of Christianity in England in the latter half of the eighteenth century. His testimony was simple yet powerful: If God could save someone as pathetic as himself and through the power of mercy could give him a heart of love, He could save anyone who called upon His name.

Once in the ministry, this reformed servant of God, John Newton, developed a great love for hymns, so great that he himself wrote at least one hymn a week for years. In 1779, when he was fifty-four, he published a collection of his hymns, many containing autobiographical themes. The most enduring of these is unquestionably one of the best loved hymns:

> Amazing grace! how sweet the sound,
> That saved a wretch like me!
> I once was lost, but now am found,
> Was blind, but now I see.
>
> 'Twas grace that taught my heart to fear,
> And grace my fears relieved;
> How precious did that grace appear
> The hour I first believed!

John Newton made peace with his past guilt only by the grace of God. In his childhood years he had been unfairly rejected, and in his teenage and adult years he had become caught in a life-style of wretchedness. Trapped in an abyss of misery, he would have had no way of escape were it not for God's undying love for him. To label God's grace as merely amazing understates its magnificence.

ELEVEN

THE BIBLICAL FOUNDATION OF STABILITY

B y now the idea has been well established that our emotional/psychological needs can be satisfied only after we embrace spiritual solutions. Since the essence of our being is spirit, any solution to personal struggle that does not address the spiritual side of our being will lack full success. That is especially true in regard to dependence-independence imbalances, for spiritual solutions are at the heart of an individual's foundation of personal security.

In chapter 5 we explored how unmet needs can cause one's emotions and behavior to be too easily controlled by environmental factors, creating a reactor's pattern of living. That style of living is usually manifested by the tendency to be too worried about others' opinions or the tendency to become too detached from others. In either case, the person's foundation of stability is insecure because it is derived from human sources rather than from a God-inspired pattern of thought.

Therefore, if a dependence-independence imbalance is to be corrected, a biblical foundation for stability must be formed (Fig. 11.1).

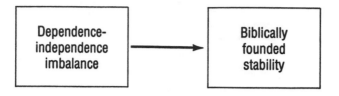

Figure 11.1

The teaching of Scripture about our value to God must become authoritative in our lives. Human opinions will still influence our emotions, but they should not be considered final. Composure should be a matter between ourselves and God, rather than being between ourselves and others.

When an individual comes to terms with his unmet needs from the past he will be ready to build on a biblical foundation of stability.

When feelings of rejection are replaced by *God's acceptance*, the individual will be less prone to be concerned about the judgments of others. Although he might experience feelings of hurt or disillusionment, they will not be dominant. An individual who clings to the hope of God's love knows that God will carry him through trying times. Because he trusts God's character, he more readily believes God's Word.

As a person learns to exercise the *privilege of choices* he breaks the confining hold of controlling or judgmental persons. Knowing that ultimately he can select his response to a circumstance, he approaches Scripture with a freshness of mind. Once he freely compares the Bible's offerings to those from human sources, he is inclined to incorporate the good news taught in the Bible. He follows the Bible's truth out of a heart of desire.

As God's *gift of strength* becomes an integral part of his personality, replacing a lack of discipline, a new foundation for security is possible for him. No longer is he prone to allowing external factors to dictate his level of composure. By studying God's promises and claiming His empowerment, he develops an internal system of stability that thrives in spite of negative circumstances.

When a *richness of experience* replaces emotional unfamiliarity, optimism comes to him more naturally. An individual who learns to understand and control negative emotions feels less threatened by circumstances that might otherwise produce momentary tension. Because he is familiar with the emotions of contentment and happiness, he is able to believe the hope offered in Scripture.

An *eternal perspective* causes an individual to rise above the setbacks of everyday living. When a person learns that God is all-powerful and offers the abundant life to anyone calling upon Him, his mind is grounded in Him rather than in the world's struggles. The result is a hunger for the truths recorded in God's written Word. Unmet needs can be resolved into a biblically founded composure and stability (fig. 11.2).

Unmet need produces:	Scripture's answer:	Results in:
Rejection Confinement Lack of discipline Emotional incompetence Spiritual immaturity	God's acceptance Privilege of choices Gift of strength Richness of experience Eternal perspective	Biblically founded stability

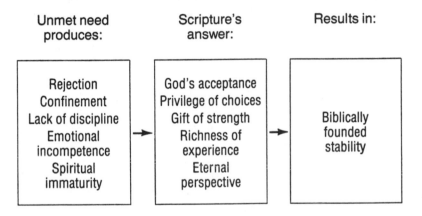

Figure 11.2

Only when we embrace the unchanging truths of Scripture can we find balance in the struggle between dependency and independence. After we claim God's Word as our foundation of stability, we will still have elements of both. We will be affected by interpersonal interaction, and at the same time we will be detached enough from the problems of others to avoid unnecessary strain. But instead of having too much dependence or too much independence, the traits of dependence and independence will be proportioned in ways that promote composure rather than tension.

STEPS TO A BIBLICAL FOUNDATION OF STABILITY

The steps necessary to build a biblical foundation of stability are not easy to implement if we have experienced tension, because tension can leave us feeling worn down. But if we persist, we can succeed in finding the desired balance.

STEP 1: ACKNOWLEDGE THE BIBLE AS TOTALLY RELIABLE

It is impossible to use biblical truth as a foundation of stability if the teachings of the Bible are considered suspect. I would not buy a home if I was told that it *might* remain standing through a rainstorm. Nor would I buy an automobile that *might* take me to my destination without catching fire. I would want to know definitively, in black-and-white terms, that I could be totally confident in the stability of such a major investment before I put any money into one.

Likewise, when I search for a source of truth that will determine my personal feelings of security, I look for something better than a book of intriguing stories. If my stability is to depend upon a particular source of truth, I want to know that that source of truth is absolute. Anything short of that will produce a tentative approach to life.

Therefore, if the Bible is to be considered an authoritative guide to personal stability, we must believe it to be absolute. It must contain no errors, must be conceptually and historically correct. If a discrepancy or error seems to be present, that discrepancy is the result of man's inability to understand rather than the result of an inherent problem in the biblical content. By adopting such an approach to Scripture, we can read it with confidence, and we can live its truths with certainty.

Second Timothy 3:16 is straightforward: "All Scripture is inspired by God and profitable for teaching, for reproof, for correction, for training in righteousness." Since God is perfect, any word given by Him is also perfect. That is particularly good news for persons looking for something reliable to depend upon. Knowing that people and circumstances eventually will disappoint, they can be relieved to find one guide that will never waver. God's truth is applicable to any person in any circumstance.

STEP 2: DON'T GIVE YOUR STABILITY TO OTHERS

How easily we succumb to the habit of allowing our moods to be controlled by others. Some people live as if each day is a blank slate waiting for the events of the day to dictate their sense of stability. If the events unfold precisely as they wish, stability is "conferred" upon them. But if events go counter to their wishes, tension erupts, distressing and disillusioning them. They cannot accurately predict if they will be composed and contented, for their composure is dependent upon what a given day will bring.

But those whose stability lies in the Word of God will allow for no such habit to dominate their personalities. Upon examining the nature of the world surrounding them, they have concluded that they cannot trust a world so stained by sin. Even friends and relatives who are committed Christians cannot be counted on to provide an atmosphere of perfect stability, because they cannot live perfectly or anticipate every need.

Although it seems pessimistic to conclude that no human can be the base of another person's stability, acknowledging this truth actually can produce a feeling of relief. It erases the sense of shock when others fail. It keeps us from being threatened by the weaknesses of others. It causes us to enjoy the positive benefits of relationships without becoming emotionally addicted to them. In essence, it produces the reminder that only God can be God. No human can bestow lasting peace upon us. Interpersonal relationships must not become burdened by impossible expectations.

This notion is welcome news for those who have been exposed to relationships that offered turmoil or disappointment. Frustrated because their desire to be content was not met, these individuals typically fantasize that happiness might have been theirs *if only* their circumstances had allowed it. They have developed the habit of allowing their moods to be determined by others, and consequently they are always riding an emotional roller coaster. When they learn to develop the habit of deriving peace from God's Word rather than from other persons, they will find that they are capable of experiencing a quality of life that they once thought was impossible.

STEP 3: DON'T RELY ON SELF FOR STABILITY

Just as it is folly to assume that others can provide a perfectly secure base of stability, so it is folly to expect to find perfect stability within oneself. Contrary to modern optimism, no person is inherently good or innately capable of discovering within himself a composure that is lasting. Speaking to the rich young ruler, Jesus explained, "No one is good except God alone" (Luke 18:19). The fact is that none of us can perform his way into a state of contentment, for each of us exhibits flaws in spite of our efforts to be on our best behavior.

If we were inherently good, we would not experience the struggles common to all individuals. We would have no impatience, lust, insensitivity, critical thinking, or insecurity. But every day, each hour, we prove that we cannot count on ourselves to do instinctively what is best. That is why a self-flattering philosophy of composure will never work.

This concept is not popular today among humanistic thinkers. Driven by the notion that man is the ultimate being, humanists assume that if we place ourselves in the right environment and focus on self-valuing ideas, we will find enough inner strength to conquer any tension the world throws at us. The philosophy is so flattering to the individual that many people are seduced into thinking that total self-sufficiency is possible. They are correct in not allowing circumstances to control them, but they are incorrect in believing in self's untapped power as the source of stability.

When Paul instructed his young protégé, Timothy, the apostle anticipated this very problem. He explained that a time would come when the public would not endure biblical doctrine: "Wanting to have their ears tickled, they will accumulate for themselves teachers in accordance to their own desires; and will turn away their ears from the truth, and will turn aside to myths" (2 Timothy 4:3-4). The message of self-elevation sounds sweet, and it tickles the ear, but it is not reliable.

STEP 4: BECOME FAMILIAR WITH SCRIPTURE

If we believe that the Bible is totally reliable and that we should build our stability on it rather than on others or on ourselves, it logically follows that we should then become familiar with the Bible. When I am going to spend some time in an unfamiliar city, the first thing I do is study a good map. There are places of interest I want to visit, but my plans will be thwarted if I intend simply to bump into my destination. Likewise, on a much grander scale, we should be motivated to study God's blueprint for living, so that we can know what right living is and how it can be realized. Personal stability expands in direct proportion to the knowledge we gain of God's will through the study of His Word.

When we study Scripture prayerfully, something happens that transcends mere intellectual stimulation. Because Scripture is the inspired Word of God, we can be assured that as we read it His Holy Spirit will speak to us and guide us with clarity and conviction. The person who enters Bible study praying to be led by God will not be disappointed.

In addition to becoming familiar with Scripture, we should read Christian books on subjects pertaining to spiritual growth. No human author can be considered infallible, but we can develop a healthy habit of serious contemplation as we are challenged to consider interpretations derived by men and women of God. When we enter this process our ideas expand, and we develop a deeper hunger to allow the mind to be absorbed in thoughts directed by God.

One of my pet peeves is the laziness exhibited by Christians who prefer to depend solely on scholars to dig out the pertinent truths from Scripture and communicate that knowledge in eloquently written books. When we form such a habit, our beliefs become passive rather than active. Our communion with God is secondhand because it is first filtered through someone else's perspective. Though it is good to have great respect for communicators of God's truth, it is unwise to depend on them to study God's Word on our behalf. We need their stimulation, but only as an adjunct to our own efforts to know God's Word.

STEP 5: FILTER ALL HUMAN MESSAGES THROUGH THE BIBLE

People who have an imbalance in the areas of dependence and independence have developed a habit of being too sensitive to the messages they receive from others. In the case of excessive dependency they worry, *What will others think?* In the case of excessive independence they think, *I'm tired of listening to everyone else, so I'll go my own way.* In either case personal stability is humanly based.

But once these persons determine to allow Scripture to be the foundation for their stability, all their experiences will be filtered through its truth. They will learn to receive what is consistent with Scripture and to disregard what is inconsistent with Scripture. A woman who has been told, "You're no good," will learn to filter that message through God's truth. Finding out that God's Word declares that God values us in spite of our sins, she will not allow the human message to have priority. A man who has always been told that he'll never accomplish anything in this world can filter that message through the Bible's promises that a believer can accomplish much through Christ. He will learn to recognize the human message as false, and it will not control him.

The importance of this filtering process for individuals with unmet needs cannot be overemphasized. Repeatedly, I have heard people who have received ill treatment or poor emotional training protest, "I don't know what to do or what to believe any more!" Not only are their minds flooded with tension-producing messages, but they are encumbered by the old habit of living in error-prone ways that originated in those messages.

Many will find it awkward to receive and incorporate Scripture's truths into their lives. One woman who suffered for years in false guilt told me she found it difficult to detach herself from the condemnation given her by other people. She said, "I know the Bible's message of cleansing is true, but it is so *different* from what I've experienced." Indeed the Bible's message is different—radically different. Yet though it may at times feel unnatural to live in its truth, we can conclude that compared to the tension produced by human experience, the Bible is the only authority that can be trusted.

STEP 6: UNDERSTAND SCRIPTURE'S EMPHASIS ON HUMAN RELATIONS

Keep in mind that the goal of finding a biblical foundation of stability should not lead us to devalue interaction. Although we should reject the control others have over our moods, we should still respect the need to maintain human ties. Interestingly, though, when we acknowledge Scripture as our source of stability, human relations take on a different quality.

When I counsel engaged couples, I usually ask, "Do you *need* to be married to each other?" Most pick up on the implication of the question and recognize my point immediately. When the Lord becomes the ultimate source of stability, human relationships are less mandatory for personal peace. By looking to Him, we will have less tendency to crave human affirmation. We will still desire interpersonal interaction, because we will be filled with God's character, which is anchored in love. We will still have an enthusiasm for personal relationships, and they will continue to play a central role in our lives. But we will already possess stability when we enter relationships, rather than entering relationships in hopes of finding stability. The motivation to maintain relationships will be desire rather than need.

Such a mind-set will help us understand more clearly the many instructions in Scripture regarding styles of interaction. We will be obedient, or patient, or forgiving, or helpful to others, not because we hope our actions will cause us to become whole, but because we wish to communicate a wholeness already found in the Lord. Our dependency will be balanced, for we will maintain closeness to others even as we maintain independence of initiative.

The person whose dependency is balanced will read Scripture less dogmatically. He will not view its instructions in obligatory terms. Rather, he will perceive the Scriptures as giving loving encouragement from a Father who wants the best for His children. Consequently, his attempts to relate lovingly to others will be untainted by troublesome emotions or dutifully imposed compulsions.

IMPLICATION: FREED TO RELATE AS INTENDED

When we choose to allow the Bible's truth to become the foundation for our stability, we will find personal freedom. Jesus Christ succinctly made the point: "You shall know the truth, and the truth shall make you free" (John 8:32). It is important that we comprehend the context of His words. He was speaking to the religious fundamentalists of the day, who needed to recognize that the only true judgment of anyone's character was that which originated from God. He then explained that He Himself was the embodiment of that truth. Therefore, anything He said or did was rightly interpreted as a direct message from God. The way to lasting peace was to invite Him to be Lord and Master of one's life and to follow His teachings.

Such a message was desperately needed by His audience, for they had been attempting to secure stability with God by human effort. They assumed that if they could live correctly, perform the appropriate rituals, and maintain an impeccable reputation, they would find peace. But of course, Jesus could see that in their hearts they were anything but peaceful.

Two thousand years have come and gone since Christ spoke those words. Our culture is far different from that of Jesus' audience. But human nature and personal needs are the same. We, too, have been fooled into believing that if we maintain the proper public image, do what is correct, and create a favorable impression, we will find stability. But in truth, such an assumption merely locks us into worries about failure, rejection, and weakness. We have the same need today that Jesus' listeners had to let the truth of Jesus Christ be the *sole* foundation of personal stability.

The freedom found in commitment to Christ enables an individual to pursue a course of life that does not waver. Though he may have had a history of unpredictable or rocky relationships, he can still be stable. Whether the world is friendly to him or antagonistic, supportive or unconcerned, encouraging or critical, stress producing or calm, he can still find peace. God never changes, and His plan is applicable to all people in any circumstance. We need not fear domination by others.

The implication of this truth is enormous. A person who has committed himself to allow God's Word to be his final guide for living can choose to disassociate himself from people and experiences that bring strife. He no longer needs to say, "You make me feel . . ." or, "If only you would . . . ," for the course of his life will not be determined by the actions and reactions of others but by his commitment to God's ways. He will have chosen a life-style of initiative rather than reaction.

A chronic pattern of reaction is common among persons whose basic needs have not been adequately met. Because they have not developed sufficient inner strength, they are usually overly sensitive to the opinions of others. Consequently, their emotions are unpredictable, for the reactions of others are sometimes difficult to interpret. Worse, their behavior is not really their own, for it is based on a guess at what others want.

When I counsel such persons, I ask them to consider what God wants them to do with their lives. Often they know the "correct" answer. They should be loving, patient, forgiving, kind, to name a few. Then I ask them to envision what life would be like if they determined to be what God wants them to be, even when the circumstances were unfavorable. At this point many waver: "You don't know how hard my husband is on me," "I've never had much self-control before, and I can't just find it overnight," "I don't know if I have the necessary concentration to do what you ask," they complain. In essence, they are saying, "I am not able to initiate good qualities, even though God's Holy Spirit is available to me."

But with the strength of God directing us, we can shed the reactor's life-style in favor of the initiator's. Daily we can let God fill us with His goodness. Daily we can determine to live a new type of life, one far different from the troubles of the past. Circumstances will certainly draw quick reactions from us, but we will not have to live in those reactions. We can allow the awakened mind we have adopted to move us just as quickly to the course God would have us take.

When I was a boy, my mother coached me before I went on outings with my friends. She did not know completely what influences would be brought to bear upon me, but she did know that she could get me thinking in terms of good behavior. She wanted those thoughts to be so emblazed on my mind that whenever I was confronted with adverse circumstances I could fall back on well-rehearsed patterns of right living. She knew that just as an accomplished actor would not dream of going on stage without rehearsing his lines, so I would not be able to engage the world successfully if I did not think in advance about the course of action I would adopt in stressful circumstances.

We can follow the same practice in attempting to break habits of dependency. Mentally rehearsing the process of letting God guide us in all circumstances will encourage us and help us maintain composure. Proverbs 15:28 advises, "The heart of the righteous ponders how to answer." By thinking in advance about the way old negative tendencies can be corralled, we can be assured that the mind can indeed take charge of emotions. We are promised that as we focus on the ways enumerated in Scripture, God will bless us with composure: "The steadfast of mind Thou wilt keep in perfect peace" (Isaiah 26:3).

Examples of taking the initiative in potentially difficult circumstances are plentiful. An adult daughter can spend time in prayer before she visits a father who has been abrasive, asking God to help her be pleasant in spite of past feelings of resentment. Before a once promiscuous student attends a class reunion he can spend time picturing how he will have God's confidence if an embarrassing memory is discussed. A brother can meditate on Scripture before he meets for the first time in years with a once-estranged sibling. A parent can meditate on God's grace as he prepares for a discussion with a son who has been the focus of family quarrels.

The key reason for meditating on God's ways and applying them to our lives is to remind us that though circumstances influence the course of our lives, they do not hold ultimate power over it. We can be freed from painful emotions as we allow our personalities to be guided by God's Word. The process may not always seem natural, but with practice it can become habitual.

TWELVE

BALANCED COMPETITIVENESS

I have to admit that I suffer from an affliction common to many: competitiveness. Sporting events are a thrill for me, and I have a difficult time containing myself when the score is tight near the end of the game. I enjoy board games, too, and approach them with the attitude that if you're going to play, you might as well win! It disgusts me when I do not perform my best in an athletic competition, but a peak performance pleases me.

Such competitiveness is normal when it is kept in perspective. Having little regard for peak performance could actually indicate laziness and passive rebellion. Yet competitiveness must be handled carefully, for it can feed the worst characteristics of human nature. Most prominent of those characteristics is the tendency to be dominated either by a sense of inferiority or a sense of superiority. When a person is convinced of the absolute necessity of being the best, or he is devastated by failure, he has become guilty of applying so much pressure on himself that he has lost the ability to relate to others with a mind-set of coequality. Interaction with others can quickly become unscriptural.

Healthy competitiveness is the desire to achieve one's best with the abilities given to him by God. Unhealthy competitiveness likewise involves the desire to achieve one's best, but it is a competitiveness that gains victory at someone else's expense. Unhealthy competitiveness encourages an individual to feel satisfied when someone else is thrust into a loser's position. One person's success is automatically linked to another's difficulty. This attitude does nothing to build up the Body of Christ but instead encourages manipulation and striving for dominance.

In chapter 6 I discussed how tension can be manifested in inferiority-superiority struggles. Because of mankind's fall into sin, each person has within him instinctive insecurities that are derived from an intrinsic awareness that he falls short of God's perfect design.

During the developmental years, each person needs to be taught by his parents and church that a right relationship with Christ can resolve this tension. But the basic needs of many persons were improperly addressed as they were growing up. As a result many suffer the discouragement of feelings of inferiority, whereas others nurse an unhealthy need to find superiority through false compensation.

The good news is that when we incorporate Scripture's answers to our unmet needs, we can prepare our minds to surrender the inferiority-superiority struggle in favor of a balanced approach to competitiveness (fig. 12.1).

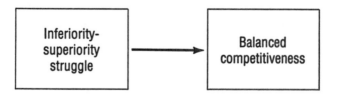

Figure 12.1

Although we will still be motivated to excel and to use our God-given gifts fully, we will not become caught in the false notion that one human being can prove himself to be superior to another. We can set aside the fear of being found less worthy than others. Our actions will be carried out in the light of the understanding that all people are coequal and of the same value to God.

God's acceptance will cause us to dismiss the idea that failure indicates low personal worth. Understanding that God has chosen to love us just as we are, we feel secure. We will recognize that it is mistaken for a person to think of himself as inferior, just as it is wrong to place ourselves above others in the search for status.

Understanding the *privilege of choices* will help us to see that we are never completely bound by difficult circumstances. Even when confinement is thrust upon us, we can still sift through options regarding our standing with others. We can choose to feel inferior, superior, or of equal value to others. Recognizing Scripture's emphasis on personal equality, we freely choose the latter.

God's *gift of strength* will cause us to know that we have the ability to handle any problem that comes our way, just as His Word promises. We can have a feeling of inner stability consistent with the stability described in Galatians 5:22-23, the description of the Spirit's fruit. We will avoid the pitfall of inferiority and the temptation of superiority, for we will recognize that inner strength is a gift of God, not something we naturally have.

Richness in experiences will give us rewarding contact with the emotions of joy, love, and pleasantness, to name a few. We will understand that those feelings are meant to be shared, that they lose richness when they are expressed from a position of superiority and are meaningless altogether when they are filtered through a mind dominated by a sense of inferiority. We will hold competitiveness in perspective, not wanting anything to get in the way of rewarding interaction with others.

An *eternal perspective* will remind us that no matter how different we are from one another in performance, none of us can claim privileged status in God's scheme. Each person falls short of God's standard of righteousness. Each person is equally in need of salvation. Excellence among men is relative, for no one is perfect.

Scripture's answers produce balanced competitiveness in our lives (fig. 12.2).

Unmet need produces:	Scripture's answer:	Results in:
Rejection Confinement Lack of discipline Emotional incompetence Spiritual immaturity	God's acceptance Privilege of choices Gift of strength Richness of experience Eternal perspective	Balanced competitiveness

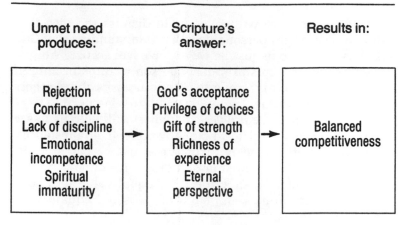

Figure 12.2

Excellence and Humility

When a person has been shaken because of a history of unmet needs, he may feel that the only way to recapture lost status is to perform in a way that shows him to be at least equal—but preferably superior—to others. We can recognize this tension by watching for various signals:

- He has a critical nature.
- He makes a consistent effort to hide personal weaknesses.
- He is overly embarrassed or unduly apologetic when he makes a mistake.
- He links self-esteem to performance.
- He is aggressive in his behavior, either through open aggression or passive aggression.
- He has difficulty proceeding slowly when he discusses personal issues. He wants quick solutions.
- Good is never good enough for him.
- He wants it to appear that he is something he is not.
- He responds to another's gain with envy.
- He is usually irritable and impatient.

We were not created by God to be thrust into unequal alignment with others, and thus it is good that we want to shed ourselves of inferiority struggles. But the key to success is not merely to sidestep a sense of inferiority; rather, it is to sidestep inferiority-superiority traps without sabotaging healthy spirit-guided relationships. We need to learn to be all that God leads us to be while still maintaining a mind-set and life-style that recognizes human coequality. We need to strike a balance between pursuing excellence and embracing humility.

SEEKING EXCELLENCE, BUT NOT MORE

Scripture encourages us to pursue excellence. In 1 Thessalonians 4:1 Paul tells believers to walk in the instruction of the Lord "that you may excel still more." Likewise, in Philippians 4:8 he exhorts the believer, "If there is any excellence and if anything worthy of praise, let your mind dwell on these things." Peter observes in his second epistle that the Christian's faith should "supply moral excellence" (1:5). Because Christianity is the embodiment of a first-rate state of mind and way of life, it follows that God desires that all that we are and do should reflect His will.

When we have lived in what might be considered a deficit situation, we may be tempted to overemphasize excelling. In fact, it is a certainty that the person who pushes too hard to excel has not correctly resolved unmet needs. His behavior reveals an insecurity that cries out: "I must appear to be more than I am to show my value." The imbalance in his life shows itself also in the way he becomes disgusted or depressed when he does not meet his goals and nourishes false pride when he succeeds.

The excellence the Scripture encourages is not tainted by insecurity and unsavory emotions. It does not rejoice in another's defeat. Rather, this excellence is spurred on by a desire to allow God's best to be in one's life so His kingdom may prosper. It is excellence that illustrates the wholeness found through Christ rather than excellence pursued to compensate for feelings of personal inadequacy.

I am acquainted with a man who openly admits that his childhood left him wanting in each of the five areas of personal needs. He remarked, "No one ever talked with me about my feelings or my spirituality. I grew up assuming that the only way to prove I was somebody was through top performance." Throughout his adolescence he pushed himself to be the best at everything he did.

He continued this pattern of behavior right up into adulthood. Then, when he was only in his early forties, he collapsed from a near-fatal heart attack. From that moment on he began to search for a new approach to life. Through counseling he discovered that his drive to achieve was not healthy. He had fooled himself into thinking that he was merely trying to do things well, whereas in reality he was obsessed with a need to mask inferiority with praiseworthy deeds.

The goal of true Christian excellence is to demonstrate the character of God. Anything else is self-serving and something other than excellence. When he explained the purpose of His good works and miracles, Jesus exposed His sole motivation for living: "That you may know and understand that the Father is in Me, and I in the Father" (John 10:38). Jesus' pursuit of excellence had nothing to do with a desire for personal acclaim but was solely for the purpose of drawing others to God. Likewise, our own efforts to excel can be guided by the goal of showing Christ to others. We can strive to do things well not so that we can gain superior status but because it is a joy to be used of God.

LIVING IN HUMILITY, NOT DEBASEMENT

The cornerstone of Jesus' character was humility. From the moment He entered humanity to the day of His death, He exuded lowliness. But paradoxically, it was this lowliness that qualified Him for greatness. Think of the many evidences of His humility. He was not born in the comfort of His parents' bedroom, but in a barn. He did not live in a cozy suburb of Jerusalem or in a wind-cooled home by the seashore, but in Nazareth, a rough, blue-collar town filled with people who barely eked out a living. His father was not a college professor or lawyer or accountant with a good income. He was a carpenter who struggled for a day's wages in a land where few things were made of wood. When He selected His inner circle, He did not conduct an extensive search of prestigious seminaries but instead chose a dozen uneducated men whose only qualification was a thorough acquaintance with hardship. In selecting His congregation for ministry, He went to the prostitutes, the lepers, and the lame. He owned no home but camped out where He could. He commanded no salary but lived by the graciousness of a kind few.

In all that He is, Jesus makes a profound statement: God is not impressed by man's pride but is pleased to honor humility. Philippians 2:5-11 eloquently summarizes God's pleasure with such a life:

> Have this attitude in yourselves which was also in Christ Jesus, who, although He existed in the form of God, did not regard equality with God a thing to be grasped, but emptied Himself, taking the form of a bond-servant, and being made in the likeness of men. And being found in appearance as a man, He humbled Himself by becoming obedient to the point of death, even death on a cross. Therefore also God highly exalted Him, and bestowed on Him the name which is above every name, that at the name of Jesus every knee should bow, of those who are in heaven, and on earth, and under the earth, and that every tongue should confess that Jesus Christ is Lord, to the glory of God the Father.

Christ's example is an object lesson in the way God desires each of us to live.

Many find humility confusing because they misunderstand what it is. People who have felt beaten down or deprived think of humility as an unwanted continuation of the sort of lowliness that fosters a sense of inadequacy. People who are accustomed to a high standard of living think that humility implies a renunciation of all forms of success. Persons at either extreme avoid embracing humility because they see it as equal to failure.

But a biblically based humility is a trait worthy of pursuit. It is a lack of self-preoccupation that enables the individual to be filled with the Holy Spirit's guidance. It does not imply inferiority to others, for Scripture is clear that in God's eyes we each have equal value. Rather, it implies grateful acceptance of God's gift of a value at the same time it implies a mind-set of obedience and submission. The humble individual experiences the sense of self-worth, but more importantly, he experiences the sense of God's worthiness in its fullness. He is so pleased to live in God's will that he sets self-will aside.

Humility is not self-debasement. It has nothing to do with self-preoccupied false guilt, for it willingly accepts God's love for the sinner. It is not to be confused with a passive, mousy disposition, nor is it akin to the lowliness that assumes everyone else is of elevated status. Humility *is* servitude—but it is voluntary servitude. Humility *is* meekness—but it is meekness accompanied with confidence. It enables a person to feel comfortable in menial tasks, yet it can exist in persons with important duties to perform.

Ultimately, humility is a blessing for those who have experienced tension. It helps them to develop a deep sense of personal security, for humility recognizes that personal worth is given by God, not acquired by performance. It helps them to see that all persons are equal, for everyone is in need of God's salvation. It helps them to obtain meaning in life, for humility fills the mind with the desire to love and to serve. It helps them see life objectively, for humility recognizes that tension is inevitable as long as sin exists.

THE IMPLICATION OF BALANCED COMPETITIVENESS

Once competitiveness is held in proper perspective, individuals are released from the worry of appearing inferior, and they are insightful enough to sidestep the falseness of superiority. When competitiveness is in check, several adjustments can be made.

ADJUSTMENT 1: OTHERS' EVALUATIONS ARE CONSIDERED LIGHTLY

Although it is foolhardy to dismiss the feedback others give us, people with balanced competitiveness are not so consumed with public opinion that they are insecure or smug. They are not obsessively concerned with "keeping their ears to the ground" to see if someone is making moves to overtake them. That game holds no sway over their emotions.

I must admit that when I discovered the futility of worrying about how others evaluated me, I felt pure relief. The discovery freed me to make my only concern what God wanted me to be—nothing more, nothing less. If others chose to be critical of me, I did not have to be overcome with insecurity, for I knew that I had been all that I could be. Nor did I have to be addicted to positive reinforcement, although I still enjoy it. I realized that the praise of others is fickle and can easily be snatched away. The adjustment in my thinking was revolutionary, for competitiveness had been the root of guilt and anger in my life, two emotions that had helped to poison my relationships with others.

When others lavish us with compliments, we can be pleased even as we recognize that we have not suddenly reached some superior status. When others treat us scornfully, we can be disappointed even as we refuse to accept a mind-set of despair. We will certainly be influenced by the evaluations others make of us, but we will be comforted in knowing that ultimately we are controlled by God's merciful opinion.

ADJUSTMENT 2: PERFORMANCES ARE NOT OBLIGATORY

When competitiveness is out of balance, performance easily becomes drudgery. Those with feelings of inferiority are panicked by the prospect of having to catch up with the crowd. They strive to achieve so that they can escape despair. Those deluded with a sense of superiority find insecurity in the falsehood that they are only as good as their latest victory. To them, defeat destroys their gains.

But persons with balanced competitiveness share neither of these motivations to perform. Understanding God's declaration of the equality of people, they live in the awareness that no performance—excellent or poor—can separate a person from others so much that God will judge him more valuable than the rest. They perform for more than self-serving motivations. They are motivated by the desire to reach constructive, well-conceived goals. They are not out to prove any-thing to others but to satisfy healthy priorities.

One woman, Kristi, told me of the lack of love in her background and the confinement of having to live within the strict mold established by her parents. "I was a straight-A student and always went beyond the call of duty to keep people happy. But I did it not because I was trying to excel in a way that would please God but because I was sure that performance was the only thing that would cause my parents to accept me."

Many others, like Kristi, can relate to the compulsiveness that accompanies the insecurity of unmet needs. But when they gain insight into how unnecessary it is to seek approval through performance, their actions acquire an entirely different feel. They are able to consult options, and thus when they do choose to perform, a freshness of mood is present. Knowing that God is pleased with good works, they do not succumb to laziness. Yet their achievements are acts of mature purpose rather than of neurotic striving. James 1:25 explains that when we embrace the freedom of God's grace we become an "effectual doer" and are blessed in all that we do.

ADJUSTMENT 3: THE OUTER SELF IS CONSISTENT WITH THE INNER SELF

An unfortunate by-product of unhealthy competitiveness is the need to look good on the outside even if that means being inconsistent with how we feel inside. A person may feel hurt and discouraged but is compelled to put on a smile and pretend all is well. A person may have experienced severe personal failure but for years never tells anyone of his troubles. A person who is not well educated on a given subject may try to pretend that he is "in the know." The need to "look good" produces a phoniness that perpetuates emotional tension and stunts spiritual growth.

When competitiveness is kept in perspective, phoniness is cut down and genuineness developed. People are willing to let others see who they are, because they are aware that we are all similar in terms of basic emotions and needs and because they have discovered that relating authentically is more important than winning. They place greater emphasis on what they are rather than what they do. More planning goes into *understanding* the inner self than into *marketing* the outer self. The net result is an individual who is so familiar with the personal, intimate matters of the personality that he is not consumed with worry over superficial externals that do little to provide meaning in life.

When we are genuine, personal relationships become more rewarding. Gone are games of manipulation and deceit. Instead, open sharing is engaged. Emotions are more freely discussed, and a cleanness of spirit is maintained. And because genuineness causes barriers to diminish, love is shared more fully and freely. James 5:16 states, "Confess your sins to one another, and pray for one another, so that you may be healed." With open, honest exchanges we minister to each other in God's love.

ADJUSTMENT 4: THE CRITICAL SPIRIT LESSENS

One of the most blatant indications that a person is struggling with feelings of inferiority is a penchant for criticism. This trait is virtually never evident in an individual attuned to the notion of human coequality. Rather, it appears when an individual thinks he lacks a competitive edge and thus desires to put other individuals down in order to elevate himself falsely. A husband may feel frustrated in his career and compensate for that frustration by being condescending to his wife and children. A woman's interaction with her father may have been troublesome, and to compensate she may frequently speak to her husband in fussy overtones. A woman who was treated like royalty when she was a child may imagine that she cannot handle any treatment short of admiration, and thus develops a finicky disposition. In any case where a person is regularly criticizing others, we can be assured that the individual is competitive to the point of feeding the inferiority-superiority tension.

People who have a balanced sense of competitiveness will have minimal struggles with criticism. They will desire excellence in themselves and in others, but their humility will remind them that all have flaws—no one can rightfully stand over another in condescension. They know that although one person's flaws may appear worse than another's, no human can claim moral superiority. They may critique themselves and others, but their critique is far different from a criticism, for it is descriptive rather than judgmental. They still discuss pluses and minuses, but in constructive rather than destructive ways.

When the critical spirit is held at bay, there is room for encouragement to gain a foothold in relationships. The encourager has no insecurity about lifting another up, because he knows that when a brother is elevated, so is he. He sprinkles his conversations liberally with compliments. He makes an all-out effort to show respect by being patient and understanding, even in the most trying of circumstances. Friendliness is prominent in him, and it is a natural rather than forced friendliness. He is inspired by the exemplary life-style of Jesus Christ and gives recognition to the need each person has for interaction with someone whose character exudes loving regard.

ADJUSTMENT 5: PERSONAL DIFFICULTIES ARE NOT THREATENING

No one likes to suffer the emotional pain of relational hardships. We have a natural aversion to being abused or rejected. But our reaction to suffering is highly influenced by how great a capacity we have for sidestepping unhealthy competitiveness. If we see troubles as threatening, we are likely to fall prey first to feelings of inadequacy, then to a powerful need to compensate through asserting superiority. But if we understand that life can be be rewarding even after we have experienced troubles, our past difficulties cannot have ultimate power.

Two sisters I know have developed radically different reactions to the problems they encountered in their childhood. Both had repeated exposure to the effects of their father's alcohol abuse. He was an unloving man and normally was withdrawn, but when he drank he would sometimes turn into a tyrant. Both girls experienced feelings of inadequacy, and both made excuses to their friends to keep them from visiting their home. As adults, however, their reaction to the past is quite different. One sister is bitter toward men, whereas the other has learned to set aside the temptation to stereotype men. One sister recalls how "burned" she was in her childhood attempts to relate to her father and will not let herself be hurt again. The other did not like the stinging rebukes of her father any better, but she does not let them control her future. That does not mean that she seeks out rejection. It means simply that her attitude is one of optimism. She believes that God will guide her into healthy ways of relating to others.

We have the promise in I Corinthians 10:13 that God will not allow anyone to be tried beyond what he is able to endure. This means that if we suffer God is able to guide us through it and to develop resilience in us. We do not need to respond to problems by cowering in fear or by nourishing dreams of revenge. We can respond to troubles with an eagerness to learn what God can teach us through them. In so doing, we can avoid unhealthy competitiveness and find the capacity to relate to everyone on an equal plane.

A NOTE TO THE READER

This book was selected by the book division of the company that publishes *Guideposts*, a monthly magazine filled with true stories of people's adventures in faith.

If you have found inspiration in this book, we think you'll find monthly help and inspiration in the exciting stories that appear in our magazine.

Guideposts is not sold on the newsstand. It's available by subscription only. And subscribing is easy. All you have to do is write Guideposts, 39 Seminary Hill Road, Carmel, New York 10512. For those with special reading needs, *Guideposts* is published in Big Print, Braille, and Talking Magazine.

When you subscribe, each month you can count on receiving exciting new evidence of God's presence and His abiding love for His people.